I Blew it I

I Blew it My Way

bebop, big bands

and Sinatra

Vic Ash

with Simon Spillett and Helen Ash

Preface by

Michael Parkinson

Northway publications

Published by Northway Publications
39 Tytherton Road, London N19 4PZ, UK.
www.northwaybooks.com

Front cover photo of Vic Ash preparing to perform with Frank
Sinatra at the pyramids in 1979. Back cover photo of Vic Ash with
the BBC Big Band in 2006 by Graham Lambourne.

A CIP record for this book is available from the British Library.

ISBN 0955090822
      9780955090820

First published 2006.

Printed and bound in Great Britain by Cromwell Press Ltd,
Trowbridge, Wiltshire.

Contents

Preface		vii
Acknowledgements		ix
1.	Early Days	1
2.	Not Tap but Bop	9
3.	You're Not Going to Play that Thing	18
4.	Vic Ash and His Sex Maniacs	23
5.	Five Gigs in One Night	32
6.	Some Americans… and Tubby	39
7.	America	48
8.	Britons in Birdland	54
9.	Send the English Cat In	62
10.	Bermuda and American Stars	78
11.	Sinatra	91
12.	Other Americans – Stars and Shows	106
13.	Marriage, Fixing, and St. Paul's	121
14.	The BBC Big Band	131
15.	Billy May and Doris Day	143
16.	Getting the Buzz	148
Chronology		157
Discography		160
Index		167

Preface

I had known Vic Ash long before he knew me or joined the band on *Parkinson*. Being a lifelong jazz fan I grew up with musicians like Kenny Baker, George Chisholm, Don Lusher, John Dankworth, Humph and Vic Ash.

They were my heroes. Still are. So when we started the *Parkinson* show way back when (1971 in fact) it was a chance to work with people like Vic, Harry Stoneham, Chris Karan and Pete Morgan who formed the nucleus of the resident band.

Together we shared the joy of welcoming great musicians, giants of jazz like Duke Ellington, Buddy Rich, Woody Herman, George Shearing, Oscar Peterson and Barney Kessel. Then the singers: Tony Bennett, Bing Crosby, Bette Midler, Paul McCartney, John Lennon, Jack Jones, Elton John, Mel Torme and countless others including the fabulous Marian Montgomery who, for a while, was our resident singer.

They were good days and they are continuing. Harry's group has grown into a big band with Laurie Holloway as its MD and many of Vic's friends playing in it.

In the thirty or more year span of the show much has changed in the world of music. What remains constant is the skill, talent and dedication of musicians like Vic Ash who are the reason why the best British musicians are among the best on the planet.

When I thank Vic for the pleasure of knowing him and hearing him play I am also paying tribute to all the men and women who have been my inspiration and joy over the many years.

Michael Parkinson
July 2006

Acknowledgements

In getting this book together I have to thank two people in particular:

There would be no book if it were not for Simon Spillett. He has a tremendous knowledge of jazz, especially the bebop era, and constantly reminded me of things I had done in the past. He also painstakingly transcribed our taped conversations, went through all my papers and made sense of their order and gave us a first draft. I am very proud of Simon. Since we first met he has developed into an outstanding saxophonist and his style has been compared to Tubby Hayes by such great players as Alan Barnes, Martin Drew and John Critchinson. He has great talents as a writer and has contributed to *Jazz Journal International* and the *Jazz Rag* and has written extensive liner notes for reissues of albums by many jazz artists. He is also working on his own biography of Tubby Hayes. Simon, thank you very much for your enthusiasm and dedication.

My wife, Helen, was the other person pushing me to write this book. Not only did she do all the typing and re-typing but she provided memories of a more personal kind and remembered stories that occurred when I was working with the big stars from the eighties onwards. I dedicate this book to her for, with her wide interest in life, she has shown me that there is also a wonderful world outside of music.

Finally, thanks to Barbara Adelman for giving us the idea for the title.

Vic Ash

1.

Early Days

'How did your parents know when you were crying?' That's the question most people ask me when they learn that both my parents were deaf. I can only think that it was instinct, the same instinct that appears to waken mothers even before their baby utters a sound.

I was born on 9 March 1930 in Whitechapel in the East End of London. At that time Whitechapel was almost entirely a Jewish area, settled by immigrants fleeing the pogroms in Eastern Europe in the previous century and the early part of the twentieth century. My grandparents had fled from Poland and Lithuania as children to start a new life free from persecution in 1880.

My mother Sarah was one of seven children. My maternal grandfather Wolf had a stall in the famous Petticoat Lane market selling fabric and he and my grandmother Ada lived in a house in Tyne Place nearby. Their children were born over a period of around ten years and my mother was the third to arrive, in 1907. After a difficult birth it was discovered that the new baby could not hear and as soon as possible she was sent to a special school for the deaf in Balham. The only thing unusual about my mother's family was heterochromia, passed down through the female side; in plain English we possessed one blue eye and one brown one.

My father Isaac also came from a family of seven children. My paternal grandparents had come from Vilna in Lithuania in the 1880s by way of Nuremburg and settled in the East End around 1900. The original name was Ask but it was changed to Ash to sound more English. They lived near Mile End and my grandfather was a barber in Fieldgate Street, Whitechapel; my two uncles followed in his footsteps. It was possibly from this branch of the family that I got my musical leanings as my cousin Maurice became a guitar player and joined a band with the improbable name of Felix Mendelssohn and his Hawaiian Serenaders. My father was born with perfect hearing but developed meningitis when he was three and was deaf from then on. He too was sent to the school for the deaf in Balham and so the story began.

Isaac and Sarah met at the school, a romance developed and in September 1928 they were married. Sarah worked for a dressmaker doing sewing and Isaac was a presser in a clothing factory. It was not until I was much older that I realised how much he was taken advantage of because of his disability. As he had no distractions because of his deafness he worked much harder than his colleagues but for less pay.

One time I phoned him at work and was very upset to hear the cry 'Tell the dummy there's a message for him.' In those days they called all deaf people 'deaf and dumb' and my parents were anything but dumb.

They used to write down what they needed in the shops. In such a close-knit community they were known by almost everyone and their lack of hearing did not present any problems. My mother's sister Annie was always at hand to sort out anything major and as I grew older I acted as interpreter. Although I knew sign language I hardly ever had to use it with my parents; we always lip read at home. With their deaf friends they used signing and my father was in fact secretary of a local deaf club.

Not so much was known about deafness in those days and though they were eager to have a baby they were anxious lest any child they might have would inherit this handicap. They went to see different doctors and were told that this was not a hereditary condition and that they should go ahead; and to their great joy I came into the world some eighteen months after their marriage. It must have been very hard for them financially. In the early 1930s, unemployment was higher than it had ever been and there were many demonstrations against authority and life was not easy. But demands were less then and it would never have occurred to people in that area to have their own bathroom, foreign holidays, a car, central heating and all the things we take for granted today.

So I began to grow up in the exciting East End of London. My memories are of a mix of people, trams, noise and a general feeling of safety with everyone seeming to be part of the same extended family. I was not aware of being different in having deaf parents but there is no doubt that if my dear Aunt Annie had not come round every day to see us, I would have grown up with a stilted way of talking. As it is, I followed her speech patterns and fitted in with the neighbourhood.

Home for us was Frostic Mansions, a tenement block that housed many other families, and it was extremely basic. Our flat was on the second floor and consisted of a tiny bedroom for me, a sitting room in which my parents slept on a pull-out couch, and a miniscule kitchenette. There was a small balcony at the back which had a toilet. I can still remember how terribly cold it was out there in the winter. On the ground floor the local greengrocer used the flat for storage and we were always greeted by the smell of decaying fruit and vegetables as we entered the block. I was too young to think that rats and mice were almost certainly there too.

There was no such thing as a bathroom in the entire building so we had to go to the public baths once a week. There were two attendants: Alf, who was a bit of a misery and expected a tip every time he gave us more hot water (even though we were paying for it) and Bill, who was a sweet guy and knew that we were all poor and thought we were paying enough for our hot water. For three old pence they filled a bath for you but if you paid sixpence you could have as much water as you liked. We could never afford sixpence and used to call out for more water – 'Hot water, number 22' – and eagerly await its arrival. Somebody made up a little song called 'Hot Water Number 22' which I often used to sing to friends' children and it is widely known to this day. It was sung to the tune of the 'Soldiers' Chorus' from *Faust* and went:

> Hot water number 22,
> Hot water number 22,
> Hot water number 22,
> Ooh, aah, that's enough. Thank you.

On one occasion, much later during the war, a V2 rocket dropped near the baths while my uncle was in there. In the shock he was seen dashing down the street clad only in his waistcoat and fob watch and chain, which must have been a very funny sight amongst all the disaster. This same uncle probably saved my life later when he happened to be passing and found me screaming with pain. He hailed a taxi – an unheard of extravagance – and rushed me to the London Hospital where I was diagnosed with peritonitis and operated on just in time.

Despite the austerity there was still much fun to be had. There I was, a pale-faced child, with a crop of black curly hair that stood up as if I'd had an electric shock, racing round absorbing all the rich life that went on. Particularly exciting was the world famous Petticoat Lane market just up the road from us, a bustling hive of activity full of colourful characters. Practically everything we needed came from there – from food and clothing to electrical items and furniture. The smell of the herrings marinading in their barrels still makes my mouth water and I shall never forget the two bagel sellers, Esther and Annie, who hated each other and would scream obscenities in Yiddish when one got a customer the other felt was rightly hers.

My parents were not especially religious but did keep the high holy days and holidays. I remember the cries of '*Chometz*' (which means food containing yeast or leavening). just before Passover when Jewish families had to dispose of anything that contained bread. For some reason, Dutch Jews would come round the houses and collect the forbidden food. I imagine it was burned, which seems a dreadful waste to me.

The only drag was school. I was never a great lover of school and will never be one of those people who say 'I wish I were back at school.' I have never wished that. Schooling in the thirties was pretty much the 3 Rs, unlike today when even five-year-olds learn computers. I was good at spelling and arithmetic but at nothing else. I must have been a bit of a wimp as I was never into sports at all and was probably too much of a good boy. I couldn't wait for school to finish.

Whilst I was dealing with my education the world's eyes were elsewhere. Hitler and the Nazis had begun their march through Europe and in 1939 war looked imminent. To reduce the risk of innocent children in London being bombed, the Government decided to send them to more rural areas far from the dangers of the big city. So the day before war broke out I became an evacuee. I was nine years old and very close to my parents and this was the first time I had ever been separated from them. I wondered how they would cope without me to interpret for them, although the rest of the family were strong support.

I was sent to a small village in Cambridgeshire, called Sutton, and one thing stands out vividly in my mind about going there. One schoolteacher had told the local children to be very careful with the new arrivals as 'these children are Jewish and they have horns.' When the local kids saw us they couldn't understand why we were just ordinary kids with no horns but just floods of tears. It sticks in my mind because we were fighting anti-semitism in Germany whilst the same ignorance was rife over here.

I was lucky in that I lived with a very kind family who had a son of my own age. On my first morning, after a tearful night, I woke to a very odd smell that I had never come across before. It was bacon frying! Coming from a Jewish family I had never come into contact with this and I was violently sick. The family were very understanding and never cooked it for me again. (I have to say that since I entered the music profession I have become very familiar with both the taste and smell of bacon and thoroughly enjoy it!)

If I had known such a word, I would have said I had come to Utopia. Being a poor city boy, this was the first time I had been to the countryside and it was a completely different world for me, far removed from the tenement blocks, the public baths, the trams and trolley buses and the street life. It was wonderful.

My parents came to visit and it was the first time that they had been to the country too and they were taken with the greenness and the space and the tranquillity. The name of the family was Murfitt and they ran a removals business. I often see large vans on the motorways with the name 'Murfitt' on the side and a window opens in my mind and I think of that warm-hearted family with whom I stayed in Sutton and wonder if any of the original family are still running the business.

However, my stay in Sutton was cut short when the Government returned many evacuees to their homes after the threatened German air-raids failed to appear. Ironically, as soon as I arrived back, the bombing of London started. I had come back just in time for the Battle of Britain, which was a thrilling sight for a ten-year-old boy. I can remember the excitement of seeing the planes in the sky as I stood outside the little concrete air-raid shelter watching the thrilling air battles and dashing back inside for safety when bits of shrapnel began falling.

Having impressionable young boys gazing skywards as the bombs rained down was too much for the Government, however, so once again I was evacuated.

This time I was sent to Leicester, which seems an odd choice as it was an industrial town. Once more the bombs were falling shortly after my arrival! I have since learned that many children had dreadful experiences as evacuees but I was a lucky child because, as in Sutton, I lived with a most wonderful family called Goodliffe who looked after me well.

The war didn't last for ever and I was back in London for VE day. I remember hearing the overwhelming cheering on the radio and the incredible street parties. Perhaps we celebrated that much more in the East End as the Blitz had destroyed so much of the area, which would change in the coming years. New buildings would replace the old disused ones and the docks, once the heartland of London and a major economic asset, would disappear completely. All that was in the future but I, as a fifteen-year-old, had already found a passion that consumed every moment of the present.

2

Not Tap but Bop

As I passed into my teens I became very conscious of the large numbers of American servicemen around. Previously I had only heard American accents at the cinema.

Even though my parents were deaf, we would all go to the cinema whenever we could afford it, especially if there was a Fred Astaire and Gingers Rogers movie showing. You didn't have to hear to appreciate and enjoy their amazing talent. We could all appreciate these films and I was completely overwhelmed by Fred Astaire. To watch him dance was breathtaking. He was a virtuoso, a pure genius who made even the most complex routines appear graceful, easy, elegant and smooth. With these films, I absorbed the marvellous songs by composers like Berlin, Gershwin, Porter and Kern which, in my opinion, have never been equalled. I wanted to be a tap dancer like Fred Astaire, but I looked at myself in the mirror with my mop of curly hair and glasses and realised, 'Vic Ash, there's no way you're going to be a tap dancer.' So my glamorous dancing aspirations were quickly over, although I remain an Astaire fan to this day and cherish the chance I had to play with this outstanding artist many years later.

My Aunt Annie had bought me a radio when I was seven, so I became familiar with the sound of the dance bands playing those wonderful melodies and I used to be a regular at the record stall in Petticoat Lane. Every Sunday a crowd of youngsters would surround the stall and marvel at the new music coming out of the wind-up gramophone. It was here I first heard the Benny Goodman small groups with Lionel Hampton and I was stunned by the speed, agility and swing of Goodman's clarinet playing on tunes like 'Avalon', which on the old three-minute 78s was over all too soon. This was the same kind of feeling I had when watching Fred Astaire. I was drawn to it, fascinated by it. Another record that mesmerised me was 'Caldonia' by Woody Herman's band. The power, the swing and the confidence of it all captivated me and I became a dedicated jazz fan.

In the days before rock and roll and juvenile delinquency, many youngsters joined youth clubs and there were lots of them in the East End. Thanks for this must go to a local man, Basil Henriques, who thought it a good idea to invest in the welfare of the young. These clubs became refuges for all kinds of teenagers with a wide variety of talents and futures, who would get together to play snooker, listen to records, do drama and other activities. In 1944 I joined the Oxford and St George's Club. Members of this club at different times included the comedians Mike and Bernie Winters and the world famous hair stylist Vidal Sassoon.

At the club there was a weekly music class and one evening I wandered in and picked up a clarinet that was not being used. I might not have been able to be a Fred Astaire but surely I could be a Benny Goodman! The following week

I arrived early at the class to lay claim to the clarinet.

We had a music teacher who showed us the basics of music and we were lent books to take home and study. I soon showed a real aptitude for the instrument and the teacher took the unusual step of letting me take the clarinet home with me. I couldn't wait to get home and practise. The clarinet became my life. I was a quick learner and played whenever I had the chance.

My parents were fascinated by it. They would put their hands on it and feel the vibrations as I blew and they were so happy to see me so happy. There were no complaints from the other tenants when I practised and the only setback came when the club needed the clarinet back for other students. My parents could see how depressed I was and they saved any money they could hoard until they had amassed £8. This was a lot of money at the time and I became the proud owner of a Boosey and Hawkes clarinet.

Many of my friends were playing instruments too. My best pal at that time was Lennie Conway and he had got hold of a tenor sax and another mate, Lennie Breslaw, had turned to the drums and would later work professionally with Tubby Hayes and Bobby Wellins as well as me. We had informal jazz sessions and sometimes participating in these was trumpeter Kenny Ball, whose career took him to the top of the pop charts in the 1960s. We all worshipped the big American swing stars and occasionally got the opportunity to meet local heroes like Ronnie Scott who, although not much older than me, was already headed for the top of the jazz business. One time we heard that Ronnie was coming to our club and a crowd of us waited for hours for him to arrive but he never showed. I ribbed him about that, years later.

In 1945 at fifteen years of age I started work as a salesman in the East End. I began selling shirts and underwear in a wholesale firm and later went to work in a chemist shop. The money I was earning enabled me to pay for clarinet lessons. I was fortunate to be accepted as a pupil by Charles Chapman, a phenomenal woodwind technician who emphasised the importance of reading music correctly. Charles had been a theatre musician playing in the pit at Victoria Palace, but by this time teaching had become his real vocation. He was pleased with my enthusiasm and willingness to work hard and he helped me iron out some of my bad habits. I studied with him for three years and in later years I was told that he talked about me often and had a large photograph of me on the wall of his practice room – as an encouragement to other pupils.

I was absorbing every scrap of jazz I could hear. I heard it on the radio, and from recordings, including the highly coveted V-disc transcriptions which stated on the label that they were 'for Armed Forces use only'. And I heard it in person, attending gigs by the new Ted Heath orchestra. I longed to get out of the dull world of Houndsditch and into the exciting world of swing.

In the meantime I played in various ad hoc groups but, more promisingly, in a band run by Paul Heimann, a local accordionist. The small band, consisting of piano, bass, drums and clarinet, could get a Glenn Miller sound with the clarinet lead on top of the accordion, which proved very popular. At the time there were many Sunday Clubs, night-clubs that were rented out for public dances on Sunday nights, and we managed to get work at a great many of these. This was an ideal grounding for me as it introduced me to commercial music and I learned far more songs than I would have if I had remained true only to jazz. But the band format was coming perilously close to repetitiveness and I was not alone in becoming very receptive to a new kind of music that was beginning to emerge.

Charlie Parker was a name that had cropped up in the mid-forties. Few of us had heard him play, though we had heard that this alto-saxophonist had invented a new music, something fresh, something contemporary. The end of World War Two had not brought forth a magical new world. The East End was still in ruins, there was rationing and the Iron Curtain had descended, bringing with it a fear of nuclear war. From this wreckage of the old world would emerge new ideas, new buildings, new fashions, new heroes and new music.

Although musicians like Benny Goodman and Artie Shaw had always employed black players on as equal a basis as possible, it was their white faces that became known and sold records and this rankled with such talented black players as Parker, trumpeter Dizzy Gillespie, pianist Thelonious Monk and drummer Kenny Clarke. The revolution started at late night jam sessions in Harlem and elsewhere when the sidemen of the big black swing bands like those of Count Basie, Cab Calloway and Earl Hines would meet to play for kicks and try some new ideas in an informal setting. They wanted to make their jazz flow in a way that was different. They were all well versed in harmony and had been attracted to its more oblique use by players such as Art Tatum and Lester Young, among others.

This became the groundwork for a music that would fully embrace harmonies that previously had only been encountered in the work of the more ambitious classical composers of the late nineteenth and early twentieth centuries. The new wave of musicians devised ways of improvising around these advanced harmonies which gave melodies odd leaps and twists. When allied to the smoother drumming of players like Kenny Clarke it became a new language. But it was initially only understood by a few. Cab Calloway described Dizzy Gillespie's efforts as 'Chinese music' and, privately, the established swing leaders sensed the threat from this new music which they could neither understand nor perform.

The years immediately after the war saw both Parker and Gillespie explode into national, and then international, prominence and there was a small boom in interest in the music, which was called bebop. Bebop found its way to England but recordings were slow to materialise. Benny Goodman and Artie Shaw did have a try at recording some bebop, without too much success, so they tended to stay in their own groove. Parlophone, one of the most prominent of the bigger labels, issued some of the first bebop records and it was one of those black-labelled 78s that changed the course of my career.

It would have been on a Sunday, when I was huddled round the stall in Petticoat Lane, that I first heard Charlie Parker and Dizzy Gillespie. The stall owner hated their records but explained that this was a new music called Rebop. It later became bebop or bop. We could hardly believe our ears. First there was a jerky angular melody which would be almost impossible to play at the speed we were hearing it. Goodman could play fast but this was almost faster than you could think. There was a trumpet solo, weird and high, followed by an alto saxophone solo. It was complex but logical, bluesy and intense.

The bop musicians changed how we thought about music. There was dixieland, swing and now this, a new music. It seemed so much more sophisticated and developed, and the melody lines with their odd leaps and twists went through the chord changes in a way we hadn't heard before. It was strange at first, after the swing we were used to, but I quickly became an addict and Charlie Parker became my new hero, following Astaire and Goodman. It was the music of our time. The first record I bought by Bird and Dizzy was 'Shawnuff'. On the B side was 'Lover Man' sung by Sarah Vaughan with the same band. The music seemed so fresh. It was an inspiration.

Although I had been making a small reputation on the semi-pro scene, I had yet to do a real 'name' engagement but in 1948 the chance arose to work with trumpeter Nat Gonella. Nat was a big pre-war jazz star and besides being a fine musician was also a very nice guy. I worked for him for one week at the Beach Ballroom in Aberdeen and to this day I can't remember how I got the gig. Perhaps the memory is eclipsed by the first real break I got, which came shortly afterwards.

In 1948 I was still working in a warehouse in the East End, not imagining that escape was not too far away. One day I had a visit from a full-faced young man with a swathe of hair swept back off his forehead. He told me that his name was Stan Tracey and that he was going to Germany with a group to do a tour of British military bases. He said he had heard of me and wondered if I would like to go with him. Would I? I was stunned at being offered a professional job like that and I did not hesitate to say yes.

I had heard of Stan and at that time he was playing mainly accordion but he was also playing some piano and was very influenced by Thelonious Monk. He had yet to emerge as one of the most distinctive pianists of any generation and as one of the most prolific jazz composers in Britain. The group included Victor Graham on trumpet (who later wrote for *Crescendo* magazine), Cliff Drinkwater on drums and a singer called Barry Martin, who years later would be the lead in *Fiddler on the Roof* in the West End.

I was incredibly excited about doing a professional tour, going abroad for the first time and seeing new places, but my parents weren't too happy about me visiting Germany. This was just a few years after the end of the war and the horrors of the Holocaust were still emerging. My family, particularly on my mother's side, tried very hard to put me off. To me, the whole thing was a big adventure and I reacted with the insensitivity of youth, but my enthusiasm won my parents over and they told me if I felt I should go, then go.

Germany was a wasteland with masses of bomb damage and Allied military personnel everywhere. We were working for a promoter of East European extraction who continually reminded us in his thick accent that, 'Boyz, you must re-urss… ' Stan and I still laugh about this.

Our job was to entertain troops in British army and air force bases in the western zones of Germany and one such installation was located near Belsen, the notorious concentration camp. I decided I had to go there to see for myself. It was hard to believe all the horrors that had taken place there such a short time before. The camp had been thoroughly cleaned up and painted so that it now resembled simple army barracks. The ovens looked like bakers' ovens. The most vivid memory of my visit is the fact that for miles around Belsen no trees grew. All those that remained were dead and never grew again. I was told this was the result of the smoke from the crematoria. Much later in the seventies whilst I was touring with Shirley MacLaine I visited Dachau and it was once again strangely unreal. It is very hard to accept that such monstrosities could occur in a civilised world in the middle of the twentieth century.

3

You're Not Going to Play that Thing . . .

The tour over, I returned to London convinced that after six
weeks on the road in Germany I was now on the way to
becoming a professional musician. I headed straight for
Archer Street. This was a narrow back road that ran behind
the famous Windmill Theatre. The street acted as an informal open-air labour exchange where London musicians
would come to get a gig. Monday afternoon saw dozens of
musicians, most of them dance band musicians and some
of them in evening dress, huddled together, talking music,
exchanging jokes and trying to find a job. Certain band-
leaders would call out: 'Trumpeter for Palais, Wednesday
night, £5!' But when you got closer you would see the bandleader had two fingers spread on his lapel, indicating the job
was in fact worth just £2. Years before, the street had been
like that every day of the week but by the late forties this
jostling bunch only appeared on Mondays.

If you didn't get a job out of it there was always a laugh
and a joke over tea in the Harmony Inn. This cafe was run
by a Czech born immigrant called George Siptak, who

provided tea, table football and, if times were hard, a generous slate. With their brand of anarchic humour, the musicians found they could raise a laugh by turning the kind proprietor's surname back to front.

These days the street looks just the same and the old Orchestra Association building still stands. The only thing that's missing is the musicians.

After a while disillusionment set in and I came to accept that I was still far away from being able to earn my living in music so I returned to Paul Heimann's band, to the Sunday-nighters and to a new day job in a chemist shop. I played with other groups too, some good, some not, but all this work helped to strengthen my musical skills.

I learned all manner of tunes and became more proficient on the clarinet but I wouldn't have been ready to deal with some requests, like the one guitarist Ike Isaacs got. Ike had a call from a musician contractor who sounded very agitated. 'Tell me,' he began. 'Can you play oriental jazz?' Visions of Chinese instruments whirled round Ike's head. 'What exactly do you mean?' he asked cautiously. He was then told the contractor had been telephoned and asked to provide a jazz-orientated musician! Most contractors (whom we musicians refer to as fixers) are more knowledgeable, I'm glad to say.

I still kept in touch with Stan Tracey and had also got to know Ronnie Scott who, barely in his twenties, had become the country's best modern jazz saxophonist. I would run into Ronnie at a small East End taxi drivers' cafe called Barney's, which a few jazz musicians used to frequent on a Saturday night after work. Over steak and a fried egg, chips and a bagel I would ply him with questions about the jazz business. I didn't want to become a burden to him but he seemed to enjoy being with me and we occasionally met at Barney's

in the company of Baroness Nica de Koenigswater, the
eccentric English aristocrat, who would later act as a philan-
thropist to New York's modern jazz community and who
would achieve notoriety when Charlie Parker died in her
apartment in 1955.

Ronnie was idolised by up and coming jazz musicians in
the late forties. But he too had heard Parker and Gillespie
and became discontented with his place in the big swing
band of Ted Heath. At this time there was a long running feud between the British Musicians' Union and the
American Federation of Musicians, which blocked American
players from performing in the UK. The Americans could
tour France and Sweden but were simply forbidden from
playing a note in Britain, except for the US service bases.
Ronnie Scott, together with drummer Tony Crombie, flew
to New York and spent an exhilarating few weeks there.
They met Parker and his young trumpeter Miles Davis and
visited every club they could. They returned home broke but
inspired.

Later several jazz musicians took jobs on the transatlantic
liners. They would play waltzes and foxtrots during the
crossing then glory in the one day turnaround when they
would spend all night in the jazz clubs. They heard Lester
Young, Billie Holiday and Art Tatum and their understanding and confidence improved. Later I too did just one of
these trips on the *Queen Mary* and was tremendously excited
by New York and its music. I also bought myself a pair of
white socks, which were unavailable in Britain at that time!

Having seen all New York had to offer, musicians such as
Scott, John Dankworth, Tony Crombie and others decided
to pool their resources and create their own club. This was
in Windmill Street and was called the Club Eleven after the

eleven founder members. It had two resident bands – one led by Ronnie and the other by John Dankworth – and became the only place in Britain in the late forties where bebop could be heard.

For a venture that existed more on luck and spirit than it did on hard cash, the club acquired a European reputation and occasional American visitors, stopping over in London, would drop in. Miles Davis, Ella Fitzgerald, Benny Goodman and Gillespie pianist John Lewis all called by to catch the music and were enthusiastic about the local talent.

I couldn't afford to make many visits to the West End but I did manage to get to the Club Eleven on a few occasions and it was always tremendously exciting to be there in this smoky, dingy, crowded room. I did get to know a few of the musicians at the club, like trumpet players Leon Calvert and Hank Shaw. I also got to know Johnny Rogers, who was the original bebop altoist in this country. And of course Ronnie himself would always say hello.

At this time the clarinet was not known at all in modern jazz. I knew that there was a young clarinet player in the States called Buddy de Franco who was playing modern jazz and this spurred me on to play it over here. So one evening I decided to go down to the club and try and sit in on a number. I asked Ronnie if I could play and, after eying my little case, he said, 'Wait until we play a blues and then come up and play.'

So I stood to the side of the band, my heart thumping. Eventually Ronnie gave me the signal to come up. I had just begun to open my case and assemble the clarinet when Tony Crombie leaned across the drums and said, 'You're not going to play that fucking thing, are you?'

Ronnie, quick to see my terrified face, said, 'Don't listen to him, you play.' I did, although my fingers were all thumbs and the audience was a blur, and afterwards Ronnie congratulated me. I had acquitted myself reasonably well and for this skinny kid with the spectacles the opportunity to play with Europe's finest musicians made me feel I was at last getting there. To be fair Tony Crombie and I later became friendly and he was highly complimentary about my playing, particularly my tenor sax playing. I don't think he ever liked the sound of the clarinet in a modern setting.

4

Vic Ash and his Sex Maniacs

In 1950 I was still living in the East End of London. However with the money I was earning from music, and encouraged by the fact that petrol rationing had just ended, I was able to afford my first car, a Hillman Minx. I was also the first person in the block to own a telephone. My wonderfully supportive parents realised that I needed to be contactable and agreed to its installation and Frostic Mansions grew used to the new sound as it had done to the clarinet. I still remember the number, Bishopsgate 4194.

Soon after we got the phone it rang and I heard an unfamiliar voice asking for me. 'Hello Vic,' the caller continued. 'This is Kenny Baker. Listen, I'm forming my own band and I've heard about you and wondered if you'd be interested in joining.' My first thought was that this was a prank. Kenny was a big star with the Ted Heath band, a big name. He'd heard of me through Stan Tracey and once I realised that it was truly him, and not one of my friends playing a joke on me, I couldn't wait to say yes.

'I couldn't wait to say yes to joining the Kenny Baker band in 1950.' *Left to right*: Johnny Arthey (piano), Kenny Baker (trumpet), Vic Ash, Jimmy Skidmore and Tubby Hayes (reeds), Pete Bray (drums), Alan MacDonald (bass).

Kenny was no bop musician himself but he was one of the greatest jazz trumpeters this country has ever produced, in all idioms. He was keen to strike out on his own and give exposure to younger musicians. The one hitch was that to be a member of his group I would have to double on the alto saxophone so I bought one and practised every spare moment.

Also in the group were tenor saxophonists Jimmy Skidmore, whose style was in the Coleman Hawkins tradition and who was a much loved figure in British jazz circles until his death in the late 1990s, and a cherub-faced fifteen-year-old called Edward Brian Hayes, better known to all as

Tubby. Tubby was already a genius, a faultless sight-reader. He quickly developed into a composer and arranger, an incredible technician, fine jazz flautist and one of the greatest tenor players of the bebop era. Unfortunately his musical skills were soon to be matched by his appetite for self-destructive habits, but in 1950 his vice was solely alcohol and there was nothing very unusual in that. The amazing thing about Tubby is that, whatever he was on, it never adversely affected his playing. He was a natural and we played together many times in the years ahead but in 1950 we were both in our first professional job and in awe of Jimmy Skidmore.

Kenny had a small library of arrangements which we ran through before taking off on tour. He had bought an old, barely roadworthy van with no heater, as was usual in those days, in which to get around. It was not the most comfortable way to travel and was a hard introduction to youngsters like Tubby and me. Our first stop was at Dudley in the Midlands, after which we all piled into the van and tried to get some sleep on the way to the next stop – Dingwall, in the north of Scotland.

Our 'roadie' at the time was a real character called MacBean. His first name was George but he never used it – he was MacBean to everyone. He acted as a minder to Tubby and me in particular but kept a fatherly eye on all the guys in the band.

When we played the Manchester area we always stayed at Mother Mac's – no relation to MacBean. Mother Mac's was in a street that no longer exists but at that time the house was home to all the touring bands. It had one single bedroom for the bandleader and one large dormitory with eight beds in it, which the rest of us used for the privilege of five shillings per night each. You can imagine the grunts and groans and odours during the night!

I did my first record date with the band in July 1951 when we recorded 'I Can't Get Started' and 'I Only Have Eyes for You' for Parlophone. Recording was quite primitive back then with hardly any editing, and that's something that has changed immensely. We more or less had to get it right in one take; if an error was made, we had to do the whole thing over again. Now it is possible to record a whole album without ever assembling a whole band together in a studio. One can overdub individually if necessary, as is often the case where vocalists are involved. Many singers prefer to go into the studio and perform to previously recorded backings. Others like to have the full band behind them as they sing, as did Frank Sinatra.

On that first date besides Kenny we had Jimmy, Tubby, David Milne on piano, Al McDonald on bass and Pete Bray on drums, but the line-up of the band changed a lot over the two or so years I was in it. Jimmy Skidmore left and was replaced by Harry Klein on baritone and alto sax. Stan Tracey was in the band for a while, as was Alan Clare.

Whilst working with Kenny I was also taking other jazz gigs and I began to get reactions in the music press. The *Melody Maker* held regular readers' and critics' polls to decide which musicians their annual awards should go to. After my debut with Kenny I began to make a showing in the voting and in 1952 won the Critics Choice recommendation as one of the most promising new jazz talents. To honour the occasion the winning musicians made a record, produced by Pat Brand, the *Melody Maker* Editor, on the Esquire label. Along with me was Ralph Dollimore on piano, Ken Wray on trombone and Geoff Taylor on alto sax.

This was my first win in a poll and I was thrilled. There were many marvellous clarinet players around like Acker Bilk, Wally Fawkes, Dave Shepherd and Sandy Brown but I was the only one trying to do a modern jazz thing with the clarinet. Even Henry McKenzie stayed more or less within the Goodman idiom. So I stood out and possibly for this reason topped the *Melody Maker* polls eight times through the fifties into the early sixties. I still have all the certificates and telegrams informing me of 'yet another win'. This was an incredibly exciting time for me.

However, trying to make a living from small modern jazz groups was not an easy thing to do for anyone. Club Eleven folded and John Dankworth and Ronnie Scott went out on their own with their bands to try and make modern jazz a more commercial venture. Kenny's band also folded as he was busy working in the session world and doing solo guest appearances. My situation was no exception and in February 1953 I joined the orchestra of Vic Lewis.

Vic is a charming man with a comprehensive jazz pedigree. He'd begun as a guitarist and in the late thirties had ventured to America to meet and play with the heroes of the Chicago jazz scene, including the legendary Eddie Condon. A decade later and he'd switched his allegiance to the progressive big band sound of Stan Kenton. Kenton's bold music had caused much controversy in the USA, and in England it met with the same reaction. So in order to make a living Vic was forced to take a more moderate course and for the rest of the fifties he mixed the work of Kenton, Billy May and Glenn Miller with that of his own staff arranger Ken Thorne.

At the time I joined in 1953 there were some very well-known faces in the band. Gordon Langhorn was there, who later became known as Don Lang and led a rock 'n' roll band called the Frantic Five. Also in the trombones was Ken Wray, with whom I'd made the Critics Choice record. Sitting beside me in the alto chair was Ronnie Chamberlain, who also considered the soprano sax a useful solo instrument and would spend much of his career shuttling between Vic Lewis' band and that of Ted Heath.

Vic was always keen to feature me with just the rhythm section and the posters would read 'Vic Lewis and his Orchestra featuring the Vic Ash Quartet'. I always played clarinet with the quartet, reserving the alto for playing in the sax section.

Vic's was another touring band and we had some horrendous journeys in those pre-motorway days. We'd get into a town with maybe three or four hours to spare if we were lucky and then we'd have to search around pubs and little bed and breakfasts for somewhere to stay. It was a bit rough but we were young and it was all a great adventure. We played large venues and small venues and even, on some occasions, ice rinks in Kirkcaldy and Falkirk, where we had to play with our coats and gloves on. But regular work with Vic Lewis gave me some measure of financial security for the first time in my life and I was able to move my parents from the tenement to a flat in Stamford Hill.

This boasted two bedrooms and a bathroom entirely for our own use!

Whilst with the band I met an Icelandic promoter who asked me if I'd be interested in taking a small jazz group to Iceland to play some concerts. There was a large American air force base there and the Icelanders had grown fond of the jazz they heard broadcast on the American Armed Forces Radio. Ronnie Scott had already been out there as a

Hljómleikar

í Austurbæjarbíói, miðvikudaginn 20. maí kl. 11.15
e. h. og fimmtudaginn 21. maí kl. 11.15 e. h.

Aðgöngumiðar seldir í Hljóðfærahúsinu og
Hljóðfæraverzlun Sigríðar Helgadóttur.

SEX MANNA HLJÓMSVEIT
VIC ASH
SKIPUÐ BEZTU JAZZLEIKURUM ENGLANDS

HARRY KLEIN
Baritón- og
altó-saxófónn

VIC ASH
Klarinett

DILL JONES
Pianó

JUDY JOHNSON
Söngkona

LEON ROY
Trommur

STAN WASSER
Bassi

PRENTSMIÐJAN ODDI H.F.

Poster for 'Vic Ash and his Six Man Group' in Iceland, 1953: Harry Klein (baritone sax), Vic Ash (clarinet), Dill Jones (piano), Leon Roy (drums), Judy
Johnson (singer) and Stan Wasser (bass).

soloist but this time they wanted a full group, which he asked me to fix.

I asked Harry Klein to come on baritone sax, Dill Jones on piano, Stan Wasser on bass and Leon Roy on drums. By this time I had begun to switch from the alto to the tenor sax. The depth of the tenor appealed to me more and gradually over the years I moved almost exclusively to the larger instrument. Our singer was Judy Johnson, who had sung with Kenny Graham's Afro Cubists. Vic Lewis kindly let me off for a few weeks and the whole thing made big news in the music press. The *New Musical Express* even sent down a photographer to the airport to photograph us as we left.

The flight was uneventful until the captain announced that he was tuning into the local Icelandic radio. As the strange language filled the aircraft we could gather that they were referring to our engagements in Iceland. We were being billed as 'Vic Ash Six Man Group' (ignoring the fact that our sixth member, Judy, was very much a woman) but the translation turned it into 'Vic Ash and his Sex Maniacs'. Much to the delight of all of us, in print it was much the same – *Sex Manna Hljómsveit Vic Ash* – and I still have the poster.

The Sex Maniacs went over well at the several concerts we gave. We started in Reykjavik and did concert and club dates all over Iceland for two weeks, supported by local musicians. One local performer, Elly Viljalhms, would later come to England and record an album of standards with my group, and we had the unusual experience of hearing the familiar Kern, Gershwin and Berlin lyrics being sung in her native tongue.

Iceland was a strange country to us; not least because of the twenty-four hour daylight which played havoc with Harry Klein's sleeping arrangements. Our return flight was equally memorable as we flew over London at the same time as the coronation of Queen Elizabeth II. It was as if we were returning to a golden age... And perhaps we were.

5

Five Gigs in One Night

Britain entered a new Elizabethan era in 1953 with renewed confidence. We had become the first country to operate a jet-powered airliner with the invention of the De Havilland Comet and Edmund Hillary had become the first man to reach the peak of Mount Everest. Randolph Turpin won back the world middleweight boxing championship and England won back the Ashes after twenty years. We were at last emerging from the hardships of the Second World War and feeling proud of ourselves.

Ironically, it was the Musicians' Union problem with the American union that aided the golden age of British jazz. As we could not see our American heroes over here, fans began to appreciate the home grown talent and jazz clubs started to spring up all over London's West End. One of these was run by a father and son, Sam and Jeff Kruger, and was called the Flamingo. The Krugers' first jazz venture was at the Mapleton Hotel in Leicester Square, known as the Club M, but the Flamingo secured its own premises in Wardour Street and additionally on Saturdays they had an 'All Nighter' at which most of us jazz musicians played. The Flamingo's bright neon sign became a landmark of London night life. This was no unfurnished basement but a proper club setting which catered as much for listeners as for dancers. Every musician was happy to work there as it was the number one jazz club in London.

There were several other clubs, some of them long established, such as the Feldman Club at 100 Oxford Street. There was Studio 51, a favourite haunt of the modernists and the Florida club. This was a boom time for players like me and once I did *five* gigs in one night – the Flamingo, the Feldman, Studio 51, the Florida and the Marquee. I would play for half an hour and move on. For each gig I received £5, making the enormous total of £25 for just one night's work.

Such financial rewards led to me leaving Vic Lewis' band in 1954 and forming my own group with Eddie Thompson, a pianist who, like Dill Jones, seemed to be able to fit in to any kind of musical genre.

Often these clubs would book all-star groups and it was then that I got to play with and know many of the great faces of British jazz. One in particular is the drummer Allan Ganley. We often bring up the question but neither Allan nor I can remember exactly when we met. It was in the early fifties and would certainly have been at a jazz club.

I've always had a rapport with drummers but Allan is a very special friend and is for me the brother I never had. We've spent some wonderful musical and social times together for more than fifty years. He is still one of the finest drummers around and has developed into a talented and distinctive arranger and composer. Allan and I just hit it off from the very beginning when he was just out of the RAF. We share the same taste in music and used to spend hours listening to jazz and to Sinatra. Allan has a great sense of humour and is a very fair man. I can't recall him saying anything bad about anyone – he is always objective and doesn't just agree with me because it's what I want to hear. We socialise and I tell him everything and we speak on the phone at least twice a week. I am a member of his Big Band and we meet each other on jazz dates too. Luckily our wives like each other as well so it makes for fun times together.

Victor Feldman, God bless him, was another good friend. He had been a big star as a young child. He had been nick-named Kid Krupa and even played with Glenn Miller during the war. He is in a movie from back then in short trousers playing the drums. We got on very well and did a *Melody Maker* record session together, a concert with my group and some club dates. He was the greatest jazz musician this country has produced, as far as I am concerned, and he moved to America where he got the chance to develop his talent and work with Cannonball Adderley, Sonny Rollins and Miles Davis. He deserved his success and also benefited from the warmer climate in California as he was an asthmatic.

Somehow Victor seemed to be always laughing. When we went out to restaurants he would always find something funny in the way the menu was written or the attitude of the waiter and we would find ourselves helpless with laughter over nothing very much. The last time I saw Victor was when we had dinner together in the early eighties. He was very depressed after the sudden death of his wife Marilyn and didn't feel he could go on. He died not long afterwards. I could never forget Victor – a warm, funny man and one of the world's greatest piano and vibes players.

Another famous character I worked with was the drummer Phil Seamen. He was a very flamboyant, almost outrageous character and, although I really don't want to delve into his private life, it is no secret that he was heavily into drugs. Drugs were rife on the British jazz scene back then. There weren't many heavy addicts and it is hard to say why they did it but maybe they got frustrated and turned to stimulants to push them that extra mile. Luckily heroin and cocaine just didn't appeal to me and I could never have considered sticking a needle into myself, although I have to admit to smoking a little dope in those days.

But Phil's story isn't all doom and gloom. When he played it was quite magical and he also had a wonderful sense of humour. One time he was working in the pit for the musical *West Side Story*. In the tacit periods he'd nod off and once he awoke to the beat of a gong, stood up and calmly announced, 'Dinner is served.' This convulsed the band but rather bewildered the audience. Phil always looked gaunt and haggard but I can remember saying that he'd been going so long on the stuff he'd outlive us all. I was wrong and it got him in the end. In 1972 he died at only forty-five.

Another world class talent was Jimmy Deuchar, a soft spoken Scotsman who found prominence as the trumpeter in the original Johnny Dankworth Seven in 1950. A player with a formidable ear, his role models were the late Fats Navarro and Clifford Brown. At one gig we did together in the early sixties, at the old Ronnie Scott Club in Gerrard Street, Jimmy chose very unusual tunes which I didn't know but he'd say, 'C'mon, with your great ears you'll be fine.' And with renewed confidence I scraped by. I think Jimmy, along with Kenny Wheeler, was the greatest modern jazz trumpet player this country has ever produced.

Much more recently, I would add Gerard Presencer to this exclusive group.

I also knew Joe Harriott, who was a tremendous altoist in the tradition of Bird and Sonny Stitt. Joe was an excellent improviser and reader but he never got into the session world as so many of us did. Now I have no way of knowing but looking back I wonder if there was some racism there, as Joe was one of the few West Indian players in London at that time. Also, Joe was not a doubler, he only played the alto but what a swinging powerful player he was.

The first few times I worked with Joe were on the Jazz Today mini tours. The National Jazz Federation, a non-profit organisation run by Harold Pendleton, had seen the success that the American impresario Norman Granz had had with the travelling Jazz at the Philharmonic package and decided to introduce something similar to Britain. We had about half a dozen blowers and a rhythm section, which we would split up into groups led by various players. For the finale we all got together for a jam session. These sessions brought in musicians of the different 'schools' of jazz so that I'd find myself alongside modern jazz players like Joe Harriott as well as mainstream players like Kenny Baker, George Chisholm and Bruce Turner. Bruce was a great sax player who more or less lived on chocolate and I can never recall a time, day or night, when he wasn't eating it.

Content in our maisonette in Stamford Hill, my parents gloried in my progress. They read about me in the musical papers and now were able to see me on television every week, as part of Steve Race's band on the show *Tele-Club*. They couldn't hear me, of course, but they could certainly see me, perched behind a Perspex music stand with my name on it.

Later on in the seventies I took my parents to see a show at the Talk of the Town nightclub where I was working and also to a recording session so they could see how it all worked even if they were unable to hear it.

Around this time I made my first records as a leader, versions of old swing standards like 'Blue Room' and 'Ain't Misbehavin'' for the Melodisc label. Melodisc was a small-budget independent label which had sprung up during the bop era. Several other labels had come and gone during this period but the one I did most work for was Nixa, an arm of the Pye Company. Nixa was run by Denis Preston, a fantastic champion of jazz of all kinds, and he recorded the local stars in his own Lansdowne Studios in Notting Hill. Lansdowne still exists and when I go there to record, it is like going back forty years. Denis could not have done more than break even with his jazz recordings but hopefully he did make a lot of money later on with the Acker Bilk hit 'Stranger on the Shore'.

I did several seven-inch EPs for Nixa. One with Kenny Baker was called *Symphony in Riffs*, which had altoist Bertie King on it, Dill Jones on piano and Stan Tracey – on accordion like the early days. On one session I had Keith Christie on trombone. He was one of a little group of us who met socially – Keith, Tubby, Allan Ganley and me. Keith spent a lot of time in Ted Heath's band and also worked in Tubby's big band with Ken Wray. For my session I had Derek Smith on piano and he also did the arrangements, which included one of my pieces, 'Cinders', a blues. As if one pun were not enough he wrote a tune called 'Ash Felt'. Derek now lives in the States and is very active in movies as well as recording sessions. On drums was Phil Seamen.

Label for EP
Vic Ash Plus Four.

Phil Seamen was also with me in 1955 when I became the first post-war British modern jazz artist to record both with string accompaniment and exclusively for the American market. The arranger was Laurie Johnson, soon to become one of our most prolific composers with TV hits like *The Avengers* theme to his credit. The album was called *Love Letters* and featured only songs with 'love' in the title – 'Lover Man', 'When I Fall in Love', 'Love for Sale' and so forth. It was rather a commercial album, with little jazz on it – I just had to play the tunes and embellish around the melody. Besides the strings and Phil, we had Max Harris on piano, Sammy Stokes on bass and Laddie Busby on trombone.

I never did find out how successful it was in the States but I still have the arrangements and I wonder if it would have any value if it were reissued as a CD.

6

Some Americans . . .
and Tubby

It was during the mid-fifties that I first started working with visiting American artists. The Musicians' Union ban was still on and we were denied the opportunity of seeing American jazz groups. The only places that were exempt from the ban were US military bases and Ronnie Scott and I travelled up north to Yorkshire to see the Woody Herman band at an air force base. The *Melody Maker* printed a picture of Ronnie and me talking to Woody and it was wonderful to actually meet the man who'd made one of my favourite records: 'Caldonia', first heard at that record stall a decade earlier.

The ban ensured that no American bands or soloists could work in clubs but there was a loophole for a category referred to as 'cabaret artists'. These were considered to be more stage artistes than outright musicians so they were allowed to appear in the UK with one of their own supporting musicians. It was therefore necessary to hire local musicians to complete the group that backed the stars. The Krugers at the Flamingo secured Billie Holiday this way and the American trumpeter Chet Baker performed a concert in London under his alter ego as a vocalist.

Handling most of these visiting Americans was Harold Davison, a well-known impresario and agent, and he booked me for three separate tours with American singers.

The first was Maxine Sullivan, who was known as the 'Loch Lomond lady' after 'Loch Lomond', her hit record of the forties. She had also starred opposite Louis Armstrong in the Broadway version of Shakespeare's *A Midsummer Night's Dream* called *Swinging the Dream*. Maxine wasn't a huge draw but the tour offered me my first chance to work with a professional from the USA. One stipulation of the Union ruling was that you could only work theatres with these tours, not clubs, but we did get the chance to make a record for Parlophone, 'Boogie Woogie Maxine' backed by 'Piper in the Glen', which was along the lines of her 'Loch Lomond' disc.

The next tour Harold offered me was an even more remarkable one. It involved a month accompanying Hoagy Carmichael, the legendary composer of such melodies as 'Stardust', 'Skylark', 'Georgia on my Mind', 'Heart and Soul' – the list goes on and on. True to his public image, Carmichael was a laid back sort of guy who had mixed freely with the finest jazz talents of the twenties and thirties. Musically it was a real treat as Hoagy only brought very skeletal parts for his tunes with piano copy sheets and the odd bass part or set of chords, so we got the chance to back him freely while he sang at the piano. I suppose only jazz musicians could have done this. Hoagy seemed very happy with our work and I was thrilled when the great man auto-graphed a song sheet of 'Stardust' for me.

Hoagy was hugely popular wherever we went and towards the end of this successful tour he invited my musicians – Freddy Cambridge on bass, Benny Goodman (not that one) on drums, Pete Williams on guitar and me on clarinet – to his room at the Savoy Hotel. We sat down and Hoagy told us how much he had enjoyed the tour and asked us if we would join him, 'in a glass of something to celebrate the success. Whisky OK?' He then filled a large tumbler to the brim with Scotch and urged us to pass it around between us! I really do not know whether this was eccentricity, a bizarre joke or just downright meanness from this very wealthy star but it makes a good story and doesn't detract from his talent or from my autographed copy of 'Stardust'.

Denis Preston, ever on the lookout for an opportunity to record, wanted to commemorate this historic tour and asked me if I would do an EP of Carmichael songs. I put together a quartet and we recorded at Lansdowne studios. I had the marvellous Bill Le Sage on piano and Sammy Stokes on bass. Sammy is now well into his eighties and I speak to him every month. He retired from the music business about thirty years ago and became a painter and decorator at Middlesex Hospital in London. He now lives in Gosport, not far away from the home of the late Nat Gonella. Phil Seamen was on drums. The record was a joy to make – the only difficulty was having to select only four of Hoagy's great tunes but eventually we settled on 'Lazybones', 'Two Sleepy People', 'The Nearness of You' and 'Skylark'. This recording was a great souvenir of my time with a giant of American music.

The next American artist I was to accompany was Cab Calloway. He had earned his fame in the 1930s when, after a spell at the famous Cotton Club in Harlem, he emerged from his old image of being a less elegant, more animated version of the show's headliner Duke Ellington, and blossomed as the leader of a fine jazz orchestra. His onstage antics were complemented by a similarly outrageous dress sense with his top hat and tails and oversized white zoot suits. But like his clothes, Cab was from the swing era and he found it hard to change. He had had to scale down his big band and go into cabaret work. By the middle of the fifties

DAVIS THEATRE
CROYDON
Licensee and Managing Director — — ALFRED DAVIS

SUNDAY, 25th SEPTEMBER
at 6.0 and 8.30 p.m.

Cab Calloway

Programme - 6d.

Programme for one of Vic's concerts
with Cab Calloway, September 1955

he was hardly a draw in America and we doubted if he would go down well over here. He was cheerful as he rehearsed for the opening show with me and Stan Tracey but show time arrived and as the curtains swung back Cab gazed out at an audience of around two dozen people. He struggled through the first house and went off in tears and cancelled the second. We did a few more equally poorly attended performances and the tour was cancelled. We all got paid but it was very embarrassing for us and we all felt desperately sorry for him. In later years he did some cameo roles in films such as *The Blues Brothers* but his time had passed.

By 1956 men like Ronnie Scott, John Dankworth and Tony Crombie had been at the top of their profession for close to a decade. Players such as myself followed them and the once fickle world of modern jazz became something

ED. W. JONES.........presents.........ON THE STAGE

THE KIRCHIN BAND

PERSONNEL.

Saxes—Brian Hayden, Alan Rowe, Barry Perry, George Robinson. Trumpets—Frank Donlan, Trevor Lanigan, Ian Hamer, George Boocock. Drums—Basil Kirchin. Bass—Ashley Kozak. Piano—Johnny Patrick. Vocalist - CLYDE RAY.

Programme selected from the following :—

1 Asia Minor..BAND
2 Zing went the Strings of my Heart............Vocal—CLYDE RAY
3 Panambo..BAND
4 Take the "A" Train...BAND
5 Tweedledee Dee..Vocal—CLYDE RAY
6 Mambo Nothing...BAND
7 The Nearness of You..................................Vocal—CLYDE RAY
8 Oolyakoo...BAND
9 John and Julie...............Featuring JOHNNY PATRICK, Piano
10 Gotta be this or that...BAND
11 Cherry Pink Mambo...BAND
12 Featuring THE JAZZ GROUP
13 Lanigiro..BAND
14 The Saints..........................Featuring NORMAN BARON, Trumpet
15 Mother Goose Jumps....................................Vocal—CLYDE RAY
16 Flying Hickory...BAND
17 The Great Lie..BAND
18 Perdido..BAND
19 Minor Mambo..BAND
20 Shake, Rattle and Roll....................................Vocal—CLYDE RAY
21 Lester Leaps In..BAND

CAB CALLOWAY

His Highdehighness of Hi De Ho !

WITH

THE VIC ASH QUARTET

1   I've got my Love to keep me warm
2   The unchained Melody
3   Summer Time
4   Learning the Blues
5   St. James' Infirmary Blues

6   THE VIC ASH QUARTET
    will play a selection from their repertoire

PERSONNEL.

VIC ASH.......................Clarinet
FRED CAMBRIDGE.............Bass
BENNY GOODMAN..............Drums
STAN TRACEY..................Piano

7   Minnie the Moocher
8   Shake, Rattle and Roll
9   It ain't necessarily so
10 I can't give you anything but love, baby

THE POPULAR TELEVISION PERSONALITY—

TERRY SCOTT

LICENSED BARS OPEN IN RESTAURANT

Programme notes for a concert with Cab Calloway at the Davis Theatre in Croydon, September 1955.

more permanent and accepted. Little did we know that we were enjoying the last halcyon days of jazz before the advent of rock and roll would entice away the younger listeners, alter musical tastes and create a whole new group of musicians whose financial rewards we could not have dreamed of.

We had all done our share of discovering new talent. Don Rendell had found Ronnie Ross, the lyrical baritonist who would later work with the Modern Jazz Quartet when they toured Britain. Tommy Whittle had helped Kenny Wheeler, and so on. I can lay claim to furthering the career of Terry Shannon. I first met Terry when I guested at a club in New Cross. I instantly realised that here was an exceptionally gifted pianist. He was inspired by Horace

Silver and, like Silver, was also a wonderful accompanist, although at that time only a semi-pro. I couldn't stop telling people about Terry and soon he was appearing regularly at the Flamingo and making recordings with the likes of Ronnie Scott, Dizzy Reece and Victor Feldman. I finally enticed him to give up his day job and join my new quartet.

One of our first engagements was in February 1956 at the Second Annual Modern Jazz Festival held at the Royal Festival Hall in London. Again Harold Pendleton and the NJF had assembled the country's finest talents to perform a whole afternoon of music; my group joined a bill featuring Ronnie Scott's orchestra, the New Jazz Group co-led by Allan Ganley and Derek Smith, and the Tubby Hayes Octet. At the time I had gained considerable success with my recording of the old standard 'Cocktails for Two'. It had been aired on Jack Jackson's famous *Record Round-Up* radio programme and became something of a hit. When we played it at the concert it caused a sensation with the audience whistling, cheering and generally going wild. We turned out to be the hit of the evening and the publicity which followed the concert did us no harm at all. Part of the concert was recorded by Tony Hall for Tempo Records and they put out four of our tunes on an EP: 'Doxy' by Sonny Rollins, 'Blue Lou', 'Just One of those Things', and 'Early Morning' which Bill le Sage had written for Tony Kinsey.

That concert was a great indication of how we were able to fill the halls with audiences who wanted to hear British groups. We did get good crowds at the all-night clubs but, once the ban was lifted and the Americans started coming over, people quite understandably wanted to see them. After all, given a choice who would you want to see – Stan Getz or

Vic Ash? Not that I'm in any way comparing myself with my favourite tenor player of all time.

The following year Terry Shannon left my group to join Ronnie Scott and Tubby Hayes in their new band, the Jazz Couriers. Although I was sad to see him go, I really thought that the Couriers were the best modern jazz group that this country had ever produced and I still think so, even by today's standards. Ronnie and Tubby had tired of running their own bands and decided to pool their resources and form an out and out jazz group. Two tenor saxes and a rhythm section was already a classic line-up and Tubby was fast developing arranging and composing skills. Sometimes, by way of a change, Tubby would switch to the vibraphone, an instrument he had taken up at the instigation of Victor Feldman, and which he played with the same ease and confidence as he played the tenor. Later he added the flute.

EP from the Royal Festival Hall concert in February, 1956, Pete Elderfield, Benny Goodman, Terry Shannon, Vic Ash.

Everyone loved the Couriers. They liked to play hard and fast with the occasional slow ballad as a contrast and Ronnie and Tubby seemed to jell like one man. Tubby did all the arrangements because Ronnie, by his own admission, was lazy and only wanted to play his saxophone, play chess and do a little gambling. Drummer Bill Eyden and bassist Ron Mathewson completed the personnel and the band provided a dramatic contrast to most other groups around at the time.

I often found myself on the same bill as the Jazz Couriers and, much as I was impressed by his musicianship, I became concerned about Tubby's welfare. Back in our days with Kenny Baker, he seemed to me to drink an alarming amount, but now he was using hard drugs as a matter of course. Only in his early twenties, he would probably have laughed off any suggestion that this would all have dire effects in future; and, as I have remarked before, it did not affect his playing.

Tubby was one of the greatest jazzmen in the world. I was enormously impressed by him. I remember one night I was playing at the Flamingo and there was a big crowd there listening to the group. I was playing the tenor sax by now but still did not have the same confidence with it as I did with the clarinet. I began playing 'Royal Ascot', a tune which Tubby had written for the Jazz Couriers, and I was playing a long tenor solo when in walked Tubby. I must have been inspired that night for when I went into the band room there was Tubby waiting for me. 'Fantastic!' he said, 'I never knew you played tenor like that!' Coming from Tubby, this made me feel ten foot tall and I had a daffy grin on my face for weeks. I forgot the clarinet; all I wanted to do was get onto the tenor. Just one compliment from a giant like Tubby was all it needed to give me the confidence to go all out on the tenor sax.

Sometimes, however, his presence could have the opposite effect. Almost a year later I was playing with a group I co-led with Harry Klein called the Jazz Five at a concert at the Liverpool Empire. We were opening the bill for the Dave Brubeck Quartet and, while I was playing, I suddenly saw Tubby in the audience. I dried up and just could not get my act together at all. It was silly, of course, because we'd played together and were friends, but knowing that this incredible talent was watching and listening just made me freeze.

I often talk about Tubby and many of the younger musicians who were not around at the time ask me about him. He was a great character and his talent was overwhelming. Tubby somehow seemed to stand out in a crowd. He was an extrovert and we got on well.

I went to see him two or three days before he died in a depressing Victorian hospital ward. He had suffered heart problems, possibly caused by all the drugs he took. He was quite chirpy and seemed to be getting better but he had got very thin so we called him 'Tubey'. Probably, with modern technology, he would have lived but his light was too bright and was extinguished at the age of only thirty-eight. I think anyone who had ever been associated with jazz turned out for his funeral at Golders Green. I still miss him.

7

America

In September 1956 I made my only trip on the *Queen Mary* to New York. The ship was so enormous that I never did manage to explore all of it. The trip took five or six days and I was working in a dreadful commercial band led by a fiddle player. We had to play around three times a day and because the money was so poor the other musicians in the group were fighting for overtime. I used to pray '*Please*, no overtime,' as I hated the music so much and only endured it as a way of getting to New York, the heart of jazz.

It is hard to describe my emotions at finally arriving in New York. Years of watching movies had made its skyline more familiar than that of London and I could not believe I was actually there and seeing it. As the ship passed by the Statue of Liberty I was seized by a panic that I would not be able to see enough in only twenty-four hours. I didn't dream that I would visit New York dozens of times in the future simply for holidays and the thrill of being in that pulsating city.

It was the speed of the city that really struck me as I took my first steps off the ship. The colours of the cars were so bright, yellow cabs whizzed past, and the revolving doors were so quick that if you weren't alert you'd find yourself back where you'd started on the pavement. The store windows were like Aladdin's cave and boasted luxuries we had never imagined. All I could manage to buy, apart from the white socks (which were a symbol of cool American youth, not obtainable in England at that time), were an Ivy League tie and a box of clarinet reeds, bought from Manny's, the downtown music store once frequented by Charlie Parker. I caught some jazz at Birdland but most of the big names were out of town on tour. It didn't really matter; just the thrill of being in New York was enough for me and I have that sense of excitement to this day. I only need to see Times Square in a film or on television and I want to be back in New York.

In 1956 the Musicians' Union and the American Federation had finally come to an agreement. In order for an American band to play over here we would have to send a band to play in the United States. It was supposed to be a man for man deal but, on the first visit that I was involved in, my little group was exchanged for the whole Count Basie band. Another rule that was bent was the one that stated we were supposed to play similar venues to those the American bands were playing in Britain. In 1957, while the Basie band would pack the Royal Festival Hall or Royal Albert Hall, it would have been ridiculous to put on a virtually unknown British band at Carnegie Hall, so we ended up playing at army and air force bases.

This trip was with a slightly more commercial group I had formed called 'Vic Ash and his Music'. The first engagement for this group had been with the Mecca Ballroom people who had booked us into the Victoria Ballroom in

Nottingham. We had been booked for a trial period of a couple of weeks to see if this new jazz idea would work but it was a total disaster. There was nothing wrong with our music but the people who went to Mecca dance halls were not ready for a small jazz group – they probably still aren't – and we finished after a week.

So off we went to the States where I had naively thought, 'Hey, they're Americans, they *must* like jazz,' but that wasn't the case. We did, however, get good crowds and a warm reception. Unlike the previous year I was able to see much more jazz, as we were on tour rather than there for just one day, and when I found out that my hero Stan Getz was appearing in Boston I knew I just had to see *him*. Stan had taken his inspiration from Lester Young and developed it into a voice entirely his own. He was as comfortable riding a roller coaster bop tune as he was caressing a ballad, but it was his lyrical flair that earned him his fame and captured me. There was something about his sound that made him the jazz equivalent of Frank Sinatra, a singer I venerated and who would later play an important part in my career.

Stan was playing at a club called Storyville and, seated with drummer Cyril Sherman at a table near the stage, I eagerly awaited his appearance. To our intense disappointment Stan appeared to be stoned, continually fiddling with his reed and mouthpiece, adjusting it, re-adjusting it, his golden sound pierced with shrill squeaks.

The first set over, he seemed relieved to retire to the bar so I thought I would introduce myself to my hero. I explained that I was a British musician and great fan and offered to buy him a drink. 'Sure,' he replied, 'I'll have a brandy and coke.' As I relaxed and began to talk music, the drink arrived, and without saying a word Stan gulped it down and walked off, leaving me in mid-sentence. That was my one and only meeting with him. I saw him later in concerts in Britain and he was as marvellous as ever and he still remains my all-time favourite jazz musician.

Another great talent I saw on the trip was John Coltrane. I had heard him on his first records with Miles Davis. He had a very unorthodox style and at first I wasn't too sure of him. It was only after seeing him live that I began to appreciate what he was doing. I saw him at the Five Spot in Greenwich Village with the great Thelonious Monk. Monk would get up from the piano stool and dance while Coltrane played his unusual, fast yet beautiful music. Coltrane was the forerunner to players like Michael Brecker, who has pushed Coltrane's approach on almost unbelievably. Sometimes I find it all a bit intense but I cannot deny the genius behind it all.

Back in London and temporarily between groups, I rejoined Vic Lewis for a brief stay, this time playing not alto sax but tenor. The tenor is pitched in B-flat, the same key as the clarinet, so it made an ideal double and I had really gained confidence in using this instrument. The music press had given me strong supportive reviews which (although my personal favourite is Getz) compared my sound to Zoot Sims, Hank Mobley and Harold Land. I thought, 'If they think I sound like that I can't be bad!'

My time with Lewis passed quickly and I set about organising another band with a more ambitious line-up. The front line consisted of Ian Hamer, a bop trumpeter who doubled on flugel and the rare bass-trumpet, and Johnny Scott on alto sax. Johnny had made a name for himself on this instrument but his real love lay in composing and arranging. Between them, Ian and Johnny wrote a high percentage of our material. The group's star was another of my discoveries, Alan Branscombe, who played vibes, piano, flute and the saxophones with equal skill and was also a fine composer and arranger.

I had arty stylised music stands specially built and chocolate brown band suits tailored at Cecil Gee. We soon became a popular attraction at the London clubs and got praise from the musical press for my own new-found tenor skills and the various permutations that our multi-instrumental line-up allowed. Most praise was for Alan Branscombe, however. In spite of his habit of rarely practising he was always brilliant. He would sometimes not touch the saxophones or vibes for months, then come out and play them to perfection. Sadly Alan too had succumbed to the hard drug scene to such an extent that he had run out of available veins in his arms and was forced to inject between his toes. He too died young and is greatly missed.

In the late fifties many jazz musicians got hooked because they saw drugs as an entrée into the upper echelons of the modern jazz world. It was a risky and painful rite of passage and I am so thankful to whatever it was – upbringing, cowardice – that kept me away from this.

The Davison office got us another exchange deal in 1958 and I took a quintet featuring trumpeter Bert Courtley to the States that autumn. Bert was married to saxophonist Kathy Stobart who has only recently retired after a long stint with Humphrey Lyttleton's band, but Bert died suddenly in 1969.

We went to Birdland to catch the Basie band with its star vocalist, Joe Williams, and during the interval we introduced ourselves. Basie was only too pleased to talk and enquired after some of the musical acquaintances he had made during his trips to England. He posed for some pictures with me, Joe Williams and pianist George Shearing, who was sharing the bill.

One day we made the trek up to Harlem to see Duke Ellington's band give a concert at the legendary Apollo Theatre. His band would alternate with a movie from ten in the morning until midnight. We arrived around lunchtime towards the end of the movie in time to catch a set by the band. We were astonished to find we were the only serious members of the audience – the other dozen or so were winos and vagrants who'd sleep through anything just to keep warm. In Europe Duke's band would have filled any auditorium but, even with just us few listening, it was marvellous. We got the chance to see all those names we'd heard of like Paul Gonsalves, Harry Carney, Ray Nance, Johnny Hodges and of course the Duke himself. We were surprised though that when the band came on stage it didn't sit in organised sections but everyone sat where they liked – trumpet next to saxophone, a trombone here and there. It didn't seem to matter and we cheered so loud we almost woke up the rest of the audience!

8

Britons in Birdland

The Musicians' Union / American Federation deal worked
well after its inception and as the fifties drew to a close the
number of visiting American stars increased. They now
often arrived *en masse* in packages; Norman Granz' Jazz at the
Philharmonic returned in 1958 with Stan Getz and Sonny
Stitt, the same year as the Jazz from Carnegie Hall troupe
which boasted Zoot Sims and J. J. Johnson in its line-up. The
following year Harold Davison repeated the exercise with
George Wein's Jazz from Newport entourage, a mini-touring
version of the kind of bills that had made Wein's annual jazz
festivals at Newport in Rhode Island such a success since
their commencement in 1954.

What a treat this was for the British fans! On the bill were
Buck Clayton's band, Dizzy Gillespie's quintet, Jimmy
Rushing and the Dave Brubeck Quartet. The whole show
was compered by Willis Conover, a disc jockey on the
American Forces Network and Voice of America, who had a
rich deep voice which was ideal for radio.

The Musicians' Union had stipulated that a British group

Vic Ash with his father, Isaac, and mother, Sarah: 'my parents gloried in my progress'.

Vic with the Paul Heimann band, late-1940s. Bobby Young (vocals), Heimann (accordion), VA, Alan Simmons (bass) and Bobby Heath (drums) at the Mayfairia Club, Marble Arch. 'The small band… could get a Glenn Miller sound with the clarinet lead on top of the accordion, which proved very popular.' Photo Geo. W. Harrison.)

Setting off for the Icelandic tour, 1953: VA, Harry Klein (baritone sax), Dill Jones (piano), Judy Johnson (singer) and Stan Wasser (bass).

Left George Shearing, VA, Count Basie and Tony Scott at Birdland, New York, 1958.

Above left Receiving the *New Musical Express* clarinettist of the year award, 195. from actor Nigel Patrick. (Eric Jelly, Photography 33.)

Above right VA with 16-year-old Tubby Hayes outside Seaburn Hall, Sunderland, in 1951

Left With Lennie Conway (tenor sax) and Stan Tracey (accordion) in the la' 1940s. (Photo Geo. W. Harrison.)

bove Touring with Hoagy Carmichael in the mid-1950s. *Left to right* VA, Fred Cambridge (bass), oagy Carmichael (piano), Pete Williams (guitar), Kenny Sinfield (drums). (Brock Photography.)

elow The Jazz Five, c.1960: VA, Harry Klein (baritone sax), Bill Eyden (playing Bobby Orr's drums), alcolm Cecil (bass), Brian Dee (piano).

Above The Vic Ash Quintet, 1957: Cyril Sherman (drums), Arthur Watts (bass), Danny Termer (piano) Frank Deniz (guitar). (Flair Photography.)

Below Joe Wylie 's band enjoying the sunshine in Bermuda, 1966. *Left to right*: Wally Russell (bass) Malcolm Smith (brass), VA, Wylie (piano), Johnny Butts (drums).

Cover and extract from the programme for the Newport Jazz Festival tour of the UK, 1959.

had to appear on the bill and thus my quintet, with Ian Hamer on trumpet, had the honour of opening this show. We knew full well that we were there as a token gesture and that the audience had really come to hear the Americans. Nevertheless we did not disgrace ourselves.

Although it had not occurred to anyone that British and American musicians might actually play together, we certainly mixed socially and had lots of fun as we travelled round the country together. Dizzy Gillespie always seemed to be the focal point of the hilarity, taking every opportunity to send up his colleagues. Dizzy's band at that time was not one of his best. Since his split with Charlie Parker he had not managed to find a truly equal partner and he had tried several different combinations but to earn a living had fallen back on the classic alto sax and trumpet quintet he had helped to pioneer. His saxophonist for the trip (and for the next two years) was Leo Wright, an effective if not outstanding soloist.

The gem in the group was the pianist Junior Mance, a man with a wonderful understanding of both bop and the blues. We got quite friendly and were to meet again many years later. In 1994 I was on holiday in New York with my wife Helen and we went to an Italian restaurant called Zeno's which had jazz on Thursday nights. One evening we were there

Advertisement from the programme for the 1959 Newport Jazz Festival tour.

listening to pianist Roger Kellaway when one of our friends said casually, 'Oh, Junior Mance has just walked in; he's the guy that fixes the musicians for the jazz nights here.' I was startled and thought I would go over to him during the break to see if he remembered the Newport tour. I had hardly cleared my throat when he looked up and exclaimed, 'Vic Ash!' 'You recognise me?' I stammered. I was astounded for I hardly recognised him. He had white hair, and, as for my hair, it had completely vanished We very much enjoyed drinking together and reminiscing about that tour.

During the 1959 tour we all travelled on one bus together, except for Dave Brubeck's group. This was different from

seeing famous musicians at a club or concert; we were getting to know them first hand. Buck, Jimmy Rushing, Dizzy
and me – all our groups together. I got quite friendly with
Dizzy but the best story from this tour concerns Buck
Clayton.

In those days we had what I shall call 'lady fans' who
would follow the bands around and offer their services, not
for money but because they were such fans of jazz musicians,
especially American jazz musicians. Two or three of these
ladies became quite well-known and George Melly has mentioned them in one of his books. They are much older now,
possibly grandparents, and I wouldn't want to embarrass
them in any way by mentioning their names.

In their own country it would have been unthinkable for
the black musicians to have had white ladies throwing themselves at them and quite a few grabbed at this opportunity
with both hands. Most of them were sensible enough to take
it for what it was, a brief interlude. Buck Clayton, however,
became besotted with one of the groupies and the couple
took up more or less permanent residence at the back of the
tour bus and were quite inseparable.

I must have been a real pain in the neck in those days as I
was quite a practical joker, so, together, Willis Conover and
I cooked up a scheme. The tour took us to Scotland and we
knew that few, if any, of the musicians had been there before.
I stood up and announced that it was necessary to make a
stop at the border. I told them that under Scottish law, if a
man was travelling across the border with a lady other than
his wife, a special ritual ceremony had to be carried out or
they would be in breach of the law.

So at Gretna Green we all got out of the coach; all those
American legends, black and white, beautifully integrated as

they should be. I placed Gillespie, Rushing, Dicky Wells and all of them in a circle around Buck and his paramour. They all stood to attention as Willis Conover read a 'service' which began: 'I, Willis Conover, by the laws of Scotland temporarily invested in me, do hereby declare that you, Wilbur Buck Clayton, are now solemnly permitted...' It was actually quite a moving ceremony and I only wish I had it on tape. Buck was so emotional that he did not stop to consider how a disc jockey from New York State could suddenly find himself able to deliver Highland jurisdiction, and the tearful trumpet player and his now 'legal' lady returned to their love-nest on the back seat.

I also announced that there would be a search of the coach at the border to see if there were any illegal substances on board. Nobody said anything but we noticed a few windows being opened and small objects being hurled out. I don't think the Americans ever found out this was my idea of fun!

I spent much of 1959 back with the Vic Lewis Orchestra. This was to be his last real year of touring and he would spend the sixties immersed in agency work with, amongst others, Brian Epstein and the Beatles, making only occasional forays into recordings with all-star line-ups to remind people of his previous bandleader days.

The 1959 Vic Lewis tour included many stars of the local jazz scene as well as those who were just beginning to find their feet as performers. One such musician was a shy Canadian trumpeter named Kenny Wheeler.

Kenny had been in England since the early fifties and had been working in dance bands as well as having made inroads into the jazz world with Tommy Whittle. What made Kenny different from Jimmy Deuchar, Bert Courtley, Ian Hamer and the other modern British trumpet players was a very real unhappiness with simply playing straight-ahead bebop exactly like the American role models of the day. Kenny had fantastic technical skills and he heard a music within himself that was very different from most of his contemporaries, one which contained wide-ranging, keening melody lines and a deeply felt melancholy quite unlike that of Chet Baker, Miles Davis and Paul Desmond.

This was the first time I'd worked with him and, although I could appreciate his technical side, I really didn't appreciate his style and it took me some time to learn to understand and warm to his music. Kenny is a quiet guy who has a lovely dry sense of humour and in those days we'd sometimes share rooms together on the road. He didn't have a great deal of confidence and seemed to plough a lonely furrow, uncertain of how his music would progress. He is now recognised as one of our most original contemporary players and has recorded with such giants of the modern scene as Mike Brecker.

The British jazz scene was well supported by the BBC in those days and all the local groups did broadcasts, mainly on *Jazz Club*, a weekly radio programme presented by Alan Dell, Humphrey Lyttleton, Benny Green, Peter Clayton and David Jacobs. I did television work as well, although it wasn't necessarily jazz. One show I did called *Sunday Break* was a series of religious programmes. We'd go to various churches around the country to record them with Harry Stoneham's group, which had a small string section. Harry did all the arranging and in the seventies I worked with him again many times for the Michael Parkinson television shows.

By the end of the fifties, the Americans were beginning to appreciate the skills of British jazz musicians. John Dankworth's big band played in the US at the Newport Jazz Festival in 1959 and shortly afterwards Vic Lewis' orchestra did an American tour, which Vic asked me to join. There were many renowned jazz faces in the band: my friend Allan Ganley on drums, Keith Christie on trombone, Art Ellefson on tenor sax, Jimmy Deuchar on trumpet and Ronnie Ross on baritone sax. On piano was Dudley Moore. Back then Dudley was intent on pursuing a musical career which drew heavily on his love of pianist Errol Garner's work, but his anarchic wit could not be contained and he later became a television comedian and then a famous movie actor, while always being a fine jazz pianist. Not long into the tour I fell ill with a food bug and went into hospital. The rest of the band went out on the road but on their day off Dudley either flew or got the train back to New York to visit me and cheer me up, which I really appreciated. Dudley never did get 'big-time' in his outlook, and when I last saw him, not long before his tragic early death, he was still a mate: warm, unpretentious and always ready to offer help.

The tour mainly involved playing US forces' bases, with the occasional public date, but, in a dramatic contrast to the previous trips I had made to America, it culminated in an appearance at Birdland, the most famous jazz club in the world. We were to be the first British band to play an engagement there and naturally we were all a little nervous about this important date. Vic wanted something special for the occasion and so, the day before, on a coach hurtling through America, he turned to Jimmy Deuchar and asked him to write a tune for the Birdland gig the next night.

Not only was Jimmy a wonderful trumpet player, he was a brilliant composer and arranger who, despite having had quite a few drinks, sat in the noisy, hot, distraction-filled coach with a pencil and a ream of manuscript and settled down to the job of writing and arranging an entirely new piece. He was renowned for his ability to sketch out each part in pitch and by the end of the trip the new composition and arrangement was finished and became 'Britons in Birdland'.

The following day we rehearsed at Birdland. The whole band was in awe of the place and we felt the atmosphere of this great club where all the jazz legends like Bird and Dizzy had played. Now it was our turn and we were not without nerves. When we opened, the audience was full of musicians; I saw Buddy Rich, Zoot Sims and Al Cohn sitting out front. I felt something like a schoolboy reciting in front of the headmaster but we were all determined to give it our best effort and were very warmly received. When we got to 'Britons in Birdland' I don't think there was a single mistake on the parts.

I stayed on with Vic's band when we returned to England and we did a New Year's gig at an American air force base. It was pure luxury and the drink was flowing well. Everyone was having a good time but Vic was getting very agitated because the band was getting drunk. For some reason that night the saxes were sitting behind the trombones and suddenly out of the crook of the baritone came everything the player had imbibed that evening. The poor trombonist in front was right under this fountain and I won't forget the look on Vic's face for as long as I live. The baritone player never worked with us again.

9

Send the English Cat In

I hung out with my old friends occasionally, including Ronnie Scott. Even though Club Eleven had folded, Ronnie still had the dream of running a pure jazz club, no doubt inspired by his visits to New York's 52nd Street in the late forties. When the Jazz Couriers disbanded in late 1959 he began to set the ball rolling with the aid of his close friend Pete King. King was the business end of the partnership. As a saxophonist in most of Ronnie's pre-Couriers line-ups, he had long grown accustomed to his partner's fits of impulse. But this was different. Between them they located a basement in Soho's Gerrard Street, negotiated a rent and set about transforming it into a London landmark.

It was a brave proposition and their budget was meagre but they soon found that all manner of people were willing to lend a hand. There was also a great deal of curiosity from the local jazz community and we would pop in and out and wonder how the club could possibly survive if it were to maintain its unrelenting policy of presenting unadulterated modern jazz.

Ronnie and Pete knew that their advertising would have to be as novel as their original idea. The advert, which ran in the *Melody Maker* in the weeks up until the club opened, promised many things, not least of which was, 'The first appearance in a jazz club since the relief of Mafeking by Jack Parnell' (the ex-Ted Heath drummer whose career was taking him into more commercial areas). It was Ronnie's gag, of course, and he would spend time each week inventing new humorous advertisements such as: 'Food untouched by human hands – our chef is a gorilla,' and, 'Coming next week – Miles and the Quintet – Bernard Miles that is, he plays a fine recorder.'

Despite the humour, the seriousness of their vision shone through and the club opened to a fanfare in the *Melody Maker* in October 1959. Besides Jack Parnell and Ronnie, the opening bill showcased Tubby Hayes, Eddie Thompson, Terry Shannon and Phil Seamen. True to the proprietors' desire to help less established talents, also included was nineteen-year-old Peter King (not the same one!) who had astounded us all with his complete understanding of the art of bebop alto saxophone.

As 1960 dawned I often found myself working at Ronnie Scott's, sometimes as a guest with the young pianist Michael Garrick or with Jimmy Deuchar and whatever combination of players had been booked for the night. Happy as I was freelancing, I really wanted to return to leading my own regular group and I contacted baritone player Harry Klein to chew it over. He was in a similar situation, mixing session work and jazz gigs, and liked the idea of teaming up with me. We felt we had something unusual in the pairing of baritone and tenor saxes, which was unlike anything on the local jazz scene.

At that time there were other groups around with the word 'Jazz' in their title. I suppose it stemmed from the Jazz Messengers in the States but over here there had been the Jazz Couriers (the best), the Jazz Committee with Don Rendell and Bert Courtley, and the Jazzmakers with Allan Ganley and Ronnie Ross. We called ourselves the Jazz Five.

Our main inspirations during that era were Art Blakey and the Jazz Messengers, the Miles Davis Quintet and the Max Roach–Clifford Brown band. Clifford was the trumpet player I liked best – he played like a dream – but the favourite group of Allan Ganley and me was Horace Silver's. We had, in fact, spent our night off during the American tour with Vic Lewis seeing the Horace Silver band at the Village Vanguard in New York City.

We had a few tryouts that spring with a variety of drummers, including my old East End mate Lennie Breslaw, followed by Bill Eyden, the forceful Blakey-like drummer who had fuelled the best work of the Jazz Couriers. Bill formed part of a formidable rhythm section with pianist Brian Dee and bassist Malcolm Cecil. After Bill left to join Tubby Hayes, we got Tony Mann, who is also an excellent player.

Malcolm Cecil had been on the London jazz scene since 1957 and had briefly been in the Jazz Couriers until National Service intervened. He was a lanky, bespectacled man who possessed the unusual quirk when playing of pressing his forehead into the crest of the bass – apparently aiding his hearing. He was an electronics genius and eventually he moved to the States where he got a gig programming synthesisers for Stevie Wonder. He also built his own recording studio in Santa Monica, which is where I last saw him more than twenty years ago.

Brian Dee was the latest in what I liked to call my keyboard discoveries and to show his commitment he turned fully professional. His playing at that time was greatly influenced by Wynton Kelly, then working with Miles Davis. Brian was and still is a great an excellent accompanist to various vocalists as well as a great jazz pianist in his own right.

We made our debut doing the rounds of the London jazz clubs as well as one-nighters up and down the country. Harry and I were pleased with the band and we were hailed as the best modern jazz outfit in Britain since the Jazz Couriers. I concentrated on playing tenor and had developed a harder funkier edge. Harry's baritone playing, which had sometimes been too restrained, had been transformed into a beltingly huge-toned voice. I used my clarinet only occasionally.

In July 1960 we appeared at the Beaulieu Jazz Festival, an annual event staged in the grounds of Lord Montagu's stately home. We formed part of a bill which included modernists John Dankworth, Ronnie Scott, Joe Harriott and Tubby Hayes and also included some bands that were then enjoying the popularity of the trad jazz boom. I was able to catch up with Kenny Ball and Terry Lightfoot but, whereas backstage we modern and traditional musicians would meet, share a drink and talk shop, there existed a sharp and sometimes violent dividing line between our respective audiences.

The Jazz Five were to appear at Beaulieu in the afternoon prior to Acker Bilk's band. Acker had become a household name, his bowler hat and waistcoat image sticking in the minds of the public as the personification of British trad jazz. Acker is an excellent clarinettist – albeit in a different style to my own, and he had not yet recorded his 'Stranger on the Shore', which he did in a commercially appealing way and which would become one of the biggest instrumental hits of all time.

The modern groups were continually heckled during the afternoon as the trad fans grew increasingly restless. We went on and there were soon screams of 'WE WANT ACKER!' We played on. A few drunken fans tried to pull Harry Klein into the audience and then clambered onto the roof of the outdoor stage. We began to play 'Too Close for Comfort' (an ironic choice) and things started to go badly wrong. I called out to the group: 'Off!' And we had just managed to get off-stage when the roof collapsed. There was then a total riot and this made sensational national press headlines the next day. It did not do the image of jazz any good at all and I know that Acker would have been very embarrassed by it.

The Jazz Five got good press reviews and we worked at all the important jazz clubs: the Flamingo, the Marquee and Ronnie Scott's. Another new venue for jazz was the Bull's Head at Barnes. Albert Tolley, the manager, wanted to have jazz there. The Jazz Five was the first group he booked and we played one night a week for three weeks. It was a huge success and the Bull's Head became a respected jazz club and it still is to this day, with successive managers following Albert's lead. Jazz can be heard there seven days a week.

Jazz was pretty healthy in the early sixties. There was rock 'n' roll of course and I'd even worked with Tommy Steele who was a huge name following his discovery playing a kind of skiffle in the Two I's Club in Soho. Tommy didn't appear to have let fame go to his head and was a nice regular guy. But there were still plenty of jazz fans, young jazz fans, listening to the music, and lots of fine new musicians coming onto the scene. Tony Coe was one of them and was as versatile and talented then as he is now.

By the early sixties I was also getting into some session work. To succeed in that field it was necessary to play all the doubles. I already played the bass clarinet and I took up the flute but rarely used it for jazz, just the odd solo. There weren't many jazz flute players around then and, surprisingly, I got voted into third position in a poll on flute. Johnny Scott was using it, as was Tubby, and one of the best was Harold McNair.

Harold was a Jamaican who also played the alto sax. He was the first person over here to do the Roland Kirk 'growl' on flute and was a marvellous player. He lived round the corner from me in Sutherland Avenue, Maida Vale, at that time, and when he got ill with lung cancer in the early seventies I went to see him. He was a slim chap anyway but I just couldn't believe how skinny he had become with his illness. I was shocked when he told me, 'Look, I think I'm going to be dead in a couple of days.' What can you say to someone who says something like that to you? I was speechless.

Previously, Ronnie Scott had organised a big benefit for Harold at the club and the proceeds had given Harold and his wife the chance to go on a world cruise. He wanted to repay Ronnie's kindness and had booked four tickets for the live-by-satellite screening of the Muhammad Ali– Joe Frazier boxing match from Madison Square Garden. Harold and Hilary wanted to treat Ronnie and his then partner Mary, but Harold was too ill to go. He insisted that Hilary, Ronnie and Mary go to the fight and have a good time and tragically Harold died the same night.

With the Jazz Five we were fortunate to do tours with American artists, the first of which was Miles Davis. Harold

Davison had organised the countrywide tour but, unlike the previous Jazz from Newport tour, our group did the whole first half. I was disappointed to find that John Coltrane was not going to be in Miles' quintet on this tour, as I had really become a fan of his playing by this time, but he was replaced by Sonny Stitt. Sonny was a very humorous guy and something of a hypochondriac. He'd always carry a briefcase with him and one day he opened it in front of me and showed me the contents: it was full of vitamins, bottles of pills and cures for everything one could think of.

The rhythm section was one of the finest in jazz: pianist Wynton Kelly, bassist Paul Chambers and drummer Jimmy Cobb. Both the Davis group and the Jazz Five travelled on the same tour bus so we all got to know each other quite well and Jimmy Cobb and I quickly established a back of the coach poker school.

Miles himself was not the easiest of characters to get along with. He was moody and was very taciturn with the musical press who clamoured to interview him. As he played he would turn away from the audience in a manner that indicated rudeness or indifference, but those who knew him attributed it to shyness. He was certainly not afraid to speak his mind, often accusing various people around him of saying things they hadn't, including telling Harry Klein that my wife had called him a 'nigger'. When I tackled him about this he just laughed and said, 'I was only kidding!' I got the impression that these outbursts were pre-planned to cause controversy and maintain the Davis façade.

The Jazz Five would gather at the side of the stage and watch Davis and his group in action and we were very impressed with the rhythm section. We could also sense the uneasiness between Sonny Stitt and Davis. As brilliant as

Stitt was, he couldn't be expected to fit into Coltrane's shoes and he felt uncomfortable with the modal style of playing that Davis was then getting into and which had come as second nature to his predecessor. The music was often built upon simple scales and suited Davis' spacious melodic trumpet style but Stitt, a bebopper, was used to negotiating his way around the most convoluted harmonies and somehow seemed inappropriate for the job. Miles had picked the wrong man to substitute for Coltrane but when Sonny cut loose on a blues or his nightly ballad feature, the change of atmosphere was palpable.

This music also came as a new concept to us. One night I caught Miles seated at the piano after the show. 'Hey Vic,' he said in that hoarse voice of his. 'Whenever you're playing, whatever you're playing, everything is in C. It's all in C.' I took that with a pinch of salt and Brian Dee and I still laugh about it.

Harry and I were delighted with the reception we received on the Davis tour. Miles himself had told the *Jazz News* magazine that he thought highly of our group and several of the players had said, 'Hey, I dig your group.'

Shortly after the end of the tour we went into the studio to record an album for Tempo, the Decca subsidiary label headed by Flamingo compere and supporter of British jazz, Tony Hall. Hall had produced dozens of records by Tubby Hayes, Jimmy Deuchar, Dizzy Reece and others but, to our delight, he reserved his greatest praise for the Jazz Five's effort, calling it 'the best sounding record I ever produced'. I contributed one of my rare original compositions, a blues waltz called 'Hootin' and when the album was released in the States it was called *The Hooter* whereas over here Tempo put it out as *The Five of Us*. 'Hootin' was also released as a single

Cover of *The Five of Us* album recorded in 1960 and reissued on CD. *Left to right*: Bill Eyden (drums), Vic Ash (tenor sax, clarinet), Harry Klein (baritone sax), Malcolm Cecil (bass), Brian Dee (piano).

in the States. The album was the first on which I played tenor sax and it got some favourable reviews, likening me to Hank Mobley and applauding Harry's more enthusiastic style.

I was freelancing as well as working with the Jazz Five and doing a television show for TWW in Cardiff. The programme was called *Here Today* and the Welsh pianist Dill Jones led the resident band which had Bill Sutcliffe on bass, Benny Goodman on drums and me on clarinet. All we had to do was accompany guest artists and play one jazz number a week. One of our guests was a fine singer named Matt Monro; we became very good friends and whenever possible in future he would ask for me to be in his accompanying bands. Matt was still driving a bus for a living at that time and we would sit on the beach and he would talk about his dreams to become a full-time singer and a big star like Sinatra or Crosby. Had Matt been blessed with height and a generally more attractive (to the youngsters) appearance, I really think he could have made it as a superstar. As it was, he became a huge record-seller. He was a superb singer, the best that England has produced – that's for sure.

A year after the Miles Davis tour the Jazz Five was booked to appear on the same bill as the Dave Brubeck Quartet. By that time, for the wider public, Brubeck *was* modern jazz. His music, full of overtones of classical forms, found a ready audience among the college students and those who perceived it as the 'respectable' face of modern jazz. Musicians were often divided as to its merits, even more so when Brubeck topped the pop charts with his sideman Paul Desmond's composition 'Take Five'. The critics either loved or hated Brubeck. Steve Race was certain that he had saved jazz, but Benny Green accused Brubeck of draining the very lifeblood of the music with pompous efforts to make it something wholesome, a criticism Benny also levelled at the Modern Jazz Quartet. However, everyone was in agreement about the brilliance of Paul Desmond.

Paul was a player with the same lyrical grace as Stan Getz and Chet Baker but he had a tone unlike anyone else's. As an alto saxophonist growing up in the bop era, he had loved Charlie Parker, a sentiment that eventually became mutual, but had realised that he, as a middle-class, ex-classical clarinet student had to find a musical expression of his own.

However Brubeck's group provided Paul with the best forum in which to display his sophisticated talents.

We had already met on the 1959 Jazz from Newport tour and as the 1961 tour progressed we grew more friendly. He loved the theatre and in later years he would every once in a while fly into London to catch up with the latest productions and see his English friends. He did this very quietly and never courted publicity. He could afford to do it as the royalties for 'Take Five' were coming in thick and fast. He had a nice dry sense of humour and I enjoyed his company.

In February 1962 Harry Klein and I broke up the Jazz Five, finishing with a provincial gig at Gosport. We'd been doing various things on our own and we felt we needed a change. There was also the problem of settling the personnel after the departure of Malcolm Cecil, who had left to work at Ronnie Scott's, and Brian Dee, who had joined the new Establishment Club. For most of our last engagements our pianist was Gordon Beck. Gordon was a new kind of musician, one interested in the lonely brooding romanticism of Bill Evans, and he was not simply content to play hard bop. This eventually drew him and Kenny Wheeler together. Gordon would go on to work with the American altoist Phil Woods before the end of the decade.

I thought about forming another group and looked around for a good rhythm section but the best players were already part of established bands. In an interview with *Melody Maker* I said I would be returning to freelancing. Ironically this coincided with the end of my poll-topping years. In 1962 I won the *Melody Maker* readers poll for the eighth time but the following year I conceded the clarinet title to my friend, Sandy Brown, now no longer with us.

I used to dep in John Dankworth's orchestra from time to time and when John offered me a regular job, replacing Danny Moss, I was happy to accept. John was no stranger and we had recorded together several times as part of the all-star line-ups assembled for the *Melody Maker* polls. On one of these John played a Grafton acrylic alto saxophone, the kind which Charlie Parker was also using at the time. Not long afterwards Grafton asked me to endorse their acrylic clarinet, which was a big mistake. They gave me one and promised a great deal of publicity but when I played the thing it was dreadful, with a really unpleasant sound and I felt I was playing a bar of white chocolate!

Since forming his first orchestra, after his initial success with the Seven, Dankworth had consistently managed to retain a high jazz content within the sometimes bland world of British big bands. He was fortunate in having his wife Cleo Laine in the band, an incredibly gifted singer who enjoyed popular appeal and went on to work on stage and television as an acclaimed actress. Just prior to my joining him, John had enjoyed a massive commercial success with his version of 'African Waltz', a composition by the Canadian composer, Galt McDermott, which was to remain a staple in the band's repertoire throughout my stay.

There were always great faces in the band, including Art Ellefson, a delightful Zoot Sims-style player who was one of three Canadian musicians in the orchestra at the time, the others being Ian McDougall and Kenny Wheeler. Art and I occasionally co-ran a two-tenor quintet when our Dankworth engagements permitted. There were several off-shoot small bands that were drawn from the orchestra, a practice that our jazz-loving leader actively encouraged.

Alan Branscombe divided his time between piano and vibraphone, and John's long time associate, Eddie Harvey, a fine arranger, was in the trombone section. Kenny Napper was on bass. I already knew him from the London club scene and he later went to Holland where he became an arranger for the Hilversum Orchestra. On drums was Ronnie Stephenson, who became such a good friend that I am god-father to his son Carl Victor. Sadly Ronnie died in 2003.

Life with the band involved touring around the country but this was now done in a more civilised manner than in the old days, thanks to John's popular respectability, and we did not have the mad rush to search for somewhere to stay. The long bus journeys allowed time for great friendships to develop which have lasted to this day.

As Cleo's career was leading to her pursuing other paths away from the band, John began to feature new vocalists, the most noteworthy being Bobby Breen, a Jamaican who would occasionally double as a percussionist. One of Bobby's favourite features was the old movie song 'Laura', the final line of which is 'Laura... and she's only a dream'. For some unknown reason Bobby just could not get this right and night after night he would sing 'Laura... and she's only a fool.' The band kept whispering 'dream' to him throughout the number but 'fool' still came out. One night, poor Bobby was in such a state of agitation about this and we were all mouthing, 'Dream, dream,' at him when he came to the final line and sang 'Laura... and she's only a drool.'

John got us a day or two in Saarbrucken in Germany doing five minute recordings for television. In the studios over here when you're getting ready to record you'll hear, 'OK, everyone, quiet please,' but in Germany you got, '*Achtung.*' Well, the first time I heard this I involuntarily shouted out

'Spitfire!' That got a great laugh from the band but the German technical staff weren't too happy about it. I didn't care, so when the second take came and, '*Achtung*,' was shouted out, I again followed it with, 'Spitfire!'

On a high, I carried on until the joke wore thin and John suggested I'd better cool it. To this day when I telephone Art Ellefson I just say, '*Achtung*,' and he immediately knows who it is and answers, 'Spitfire.' Maybe musicians have an especially silly sense of humour.

During my time with Dankworth, I was offered a unique musical opportunity. In May 1963 the Ray Charles Orchestra were touring Europe and on the Parisian leg of the tour the band's star tenor saxophonist, David 'Fathead' Newman, had been arrested by French narcotics officers as part of an undercover operation. Several well-known jazz musicians were staying in a house that was being decorated; all over the outside of the house were painters who, unknown to those inside, were French drug squad officers. Suddenly they swooped in through the windows and raided the place. There was a panic to find a replacement as the French were in no hurry to accelerate Newman's release from jail.

Harold Davison's office was informed and they called me and I was as surprised to get this offer as I had been by Kenny Baker's some thirteen years before. A week later I was on stage with Ray Charles at the Olympia Theatre in Paris, a solitary white face in a sea of black ones. To say I was nervous is putting it mildly, as Charles had insisted that all Newman's solos go to 'the Englishman'. The rest of the band were very supportive and helped me to relax and I soon established a rapport with the other tenorist, James Clay.

Collectively the band was spirited and a little rough around the edges but it swung with a relaxation and drive that none of the British bands I had been in did. As the week wore on, I began to feel like a regular member of the band and I was as warmly received by the audiences as by my fellow musicians. One night I was invited to a party in one of their rooms. I had no idea what to expect. Several members of the orchestra were demonstrating non-musicianly skills with a prostitute while others were sitting around puffing at a 'hubbly bubbly'. This was a bottle with a pipe sticking out of it from which they inhaled what I think was either hashish or marijuana. Eventually I was persuaded to enter into the spirit of the evening and have a go. I took one drag and went right to sleep and awoke the next morning on the hotel room floor amid a pile of snoring bodies.

The Charles tour moved on to Great Britain and the opening concert at Hammersmith.

Everything had happened so suddenly that when the curtains opened and my white face shone out it surprised everyone, including Tubby Hayes, who was once again in the audience. One of the trumpet players introduced me to the audience with words of high praise; the *Melody Maker* and *Crescendo* both ran stories about me being the first Brit and the first white man to be in the Ray Charles Orchestra and printed a photo of me and Ray backstage together.

Ray would call me into his dressing room every evening before the show. He could never remember my name but he'd say, 'Send the English cat in.' So I'd go in and we'd chat for a few minutes. 'Don't be nervous, enjoy yourself,' he'd tell me. And I did.

Some thirty-six years later I again worked with Ray Charles in the BBC Big Band and I was astonished to discover that the first tenor part contained a high proportion of the original charts I'd played in 1963, now stained, well thumbed and faded. I even recognised one or two of my own markings. Ray was appearing with his vocal group, the Raylettes, and on their dressing room door was printed 'Mr Ray Letz'!

10

Bermuda and American Stars

When I rejoined John Dankworth we began making an album at Philips' studios at Marble Arch, London. John had written a suite for the band that was based on Charles Dickens characters. Each of the soloists had individual features and mine was a clarinet showcase called 'The Artful Dodger'. John brought in many guest stars for that album, including Tubby, Ronnie Scott, Peter King, Ronnie Ross, Tony Coe and Bobby Wellins, so the album wasn't exactly short of talent. We also had a harpist called David Snell, who later became a television and film composer.

He was also on the next album I did with John's band which featured Cleo Laine and was called *Shakespeare and All that Jazz*. John had selected several of Shakespeare's sonnets and set them to music. Some of the tracks had already been recorded on an EP which I did back in 1959 with Cleo but by 1964 John had written much more complex arrangements of the tunes. It was a real pleasure to be involved with anything John had a hand in but the following album, *The Zodiac Suite*, was even more rewarding.

As well as British guests on this one, we had American musicians and some marvellous players they were: Phil Woods, Lucky Thompson, Zoot Sims, Clark Terry and Bob Brookmeyer. They had recorded their parts in the States, overdubbing on to what we had put on tape back in London, but we did get to play alongside Clark and Bob when the BBC did a *Jazz 625* television show of *The Zodiac Suite*.

The early sixties was a time of tremendous upheaval and change. The Cuban Missile Crisis of 1962 had taken the world to the brink of a nuclear war, the Berlin wall had split that city in two, the civil rights movement in the United States had exploded into a frenzy of violent demonstration and South Africa's Sharpeville massacre shocked people everywhere. Later, there was the assassination of President Kennedy and major new breakthroughs in space exploration. And there was rock music.

From its humble beginnings this had grown into massive popularity and stars such as Jerry Lee Lewis, Bill Haley, Buddy Holly and Elvis Presley were idolised. Just as my generation had followed the post-war bop trends set by the Americans, so the British teenagers copied the rock performers – not only Presley and Holly but also Little Richard, Chuck Berry and many others. The first British rock and roll bands were often nothing more than slavish imitations of the American role models. The jazz community at first laughed off rock and roll, thinking this was just another teenage fad which would swiftly die. We were wrong. Groups like the Beatles and the Rolling Stones emerged in the sixties and modern jazz was sadly pushed down the charts to appeal, as it does today, to a minority audience. It will never compete with pop but it is good to see a new jazz audience for newcomers such as Diana Krall, whilst the old big names like

Sonny Rollins, Mike Brecker, Herbie Hancock and Chick Corea can still fill houses

Due to the advent of rock and roll, Ronnie Scott and Pete King realised that it was essential for the club's survival that it somehow secure American soloists to perform there. Pete King was determined to achieve this and had long talks with the American Federation. After much negotiation, in 1961 he created a deal by which it was possible for an American soloist to work for a month at the club and an English player would play an equivalent club in the States. Tubby Hayes was the natural choice as our ambassador to the US and King decided on Zoot Sims to be the player to inaugurate the London end of the deal. Players such as Stan Getz and Lucky Thompson followed and local jazz fans at last got the chance to see these giants in action in a relaxed club setting. Ronnie once received a letter from a dissatisfied customer who complained that Ben Webster had done more talking than playing. Ronnie's reply was that he'd rather hear Webster talk than 90 per cent of other tenorists play!

I saw Dexter Gordon there (who had one of the biggest sounds I'd heard in my life), Bill Evans, Al Cohn and Zoot Sims. Together Al and Zoot were magic. I'd already seen the two saxophonists at the Metropole in New York where they played on a little stage behind the bar but when they performed at Ronnie's I got very friendly with Al. Zoot I knew only slightly but Al and I became firm friends and I would always visit him when I was in New York. I still recall his address: 28 Jane Street. Al Cohn was unassuming, not bigtime like some top musicians, and loved telling and hearing jokes. He was simply likeable and I was a great admirer, not only of his marvellous tenor playing but of his arranging too. He wrote for Tony Bennett and many other singers.

Zoot and Al played wonderful straightahead jazz and, if you listen to any of the old albums they made together back then, they still sound as fresh today. There was even an album on which they played clarinets on one track and it sounded just the way they played tenor. It was not the usual way we know clarinet playing but there was that lovely feel they had when they performed together.

I will not forget the night in December 1963 that I went down to Ronnie's club to hear Johnny Griffin, the phenomenal tenor saxophonist. I had a small van in those days and foolishly left my Selmer Centretone clarinet and King Super 20 tenor in the van outside Ronnie's. When I came out they were gone. I was devastated. The insurance company sorted me out replacements, a Selmer Mark Six and a Buffet clarinet, which I still use to this day, but a week or so after they were stolen I began receiving calls from people who'd seen my instruments on *Police Five*, the regular crime detection television show presented by Shaw Taylor. Apparently someone had been trying to sell them in a shop in Kilburn but the owner was suspicious and reported it to the police, who passed on the information to *Police Five*. As I'd already got new instruments, the insurance company sold my old ones; the tenor went to Stan Lord, a gig sax player, and Tubby got the clarinet.

The American soloists who played at Ronnie's were only visiting, of course, but one American musician who actually did live here in the early sixties was Bill Russo. Bill was an ex-Stan Kenton arranger who decided he'd like to form a British rehearsal band to play his charts as well as those of some other arrangers he had befriended in this country, like Richard Peaslee, Kenny Wheeler and Patrick Gower. Bill was a nice man and when I joined his orchestra we got together socially as well as musically. It was a band full of familiar faces, including Keith Christie, Tony Kinsey and Duncan Lamont, and we all enjoyed working on his challenging charts, which were sometimes quite complex as you'd expect from a man of his intellect. Bill lived in Holland Park so we rehearsed just around the corner at Lansdowne Studios or at Hammersmith Town Hall.

Although it started as a rehearsal band, we did do some public concerts of Bill's big works like *The Stonehenge Suite* and his opera *The Land of Milk and Honey*, for which he added Annie Ross and Bobby Breen to sing his lyrics. Denis Preston recorded the band and the album was released as *Stonehenge*. After a few years Bill went back to the States but he returned to the UK to conduct the BBC Big Band in 2003, a few months before his death, so we were able to catch up on old times.

The Bill Russo London Jazz Orchestra wasn't a regular thing and I was still working with John Dankworth's band. John had already scored a few films and it was with his orchestra that I did my first film work, recording four soundtracks. The first was *The Servant*, then *Darling*, *Modesty Blaise* and *Morgan – A Suitable Case for Treatment*.

On some of these sessions I was booked to play along with Jack Brymer. Jack was probably the greatest classical clarinettist in the country and certainly one of the top few worldwide. John would always book Jack to play First Clarinet but for a couple of times, with my readiness for a joke, I got there first and sat in the First Clarinet chair. Jack is a very modest guy and he would simply walk in and sit in the Second Clarinet chair. Then I began to worry in case Jack got his own back and forced me to play the First Clarinet part. Knowing he had Jack Brymer there, John would write what we call 'flyshit': lots of notes, fast complex cadenzas, really difficult stuff. And I didn't want to have to play it! Jack would say to me, 'You can do this.' But even if I could it would have taken a lot longer than when Jack did it.

There is a kind of mutual admiration society between jazz and classical musicians. They think what we do with improvisation is amazing and we think that their technique is amazing. Jack was fascinated with jazz and I was equally amazed at his technique. Whenever I asked him he'd give me some tips and some different mouthpieces to try out.

Over the years I played on several other film scores, including *Wild Geese* (with Roy Budd), *For Your Eyes Only* (the only James Bond film up to that point that was scored by Bill Conti), *84 Charing Cross Road* and the cartoon movie *All Dogs Go to Heaven* on which I got to work with the legendary Ralph Burns. I particularly enjoyed doing *Stepping Out* with Liza Minnelli. All these movies, of course, involved playing on the soundtrack only, but I did appear in one. That was *Steptoe and Son* and it can often be seen on television. You can see me playing alto behind a stripper in a sleazy club!

When I wasn't working I could often be found in Ronnie Scott's and one night in spring 1966 I went there with the brilliant young drummer from the Dankworth band, Johnny Butts, to catch some music and say hello to Ronnie and Pete. We ran into drummer Kenny Harris, an old acquaintance who then lived in Bermuda but was back in England to visit old friends and to do a little recruiting for fellow musician Joe Wylie, who led a band at the de luxe Hamilton Princess Hotel in Bermuda. He asked me and Johnny how we would feel about working in Bermuda. We didn't take this as a serious enquiry because Bermuda was the height of luxury, not to be visited by 'ordinary' people. Joe Wylie had asked Kenny to find a drummer and woodwind player to replace those he had and the pay on offer was the magnificent sum of £50 a week. This was incredible money in 1966, even more so when we were told Bermuda had no income tax. Kenny told us that the deal was to go over for six months and if we liked it we could stay on.

Neither Johnny nor I needed much persuasion. Dankworth's band and the jazz scene were beginning to be affected by the popularity of pop groups. The Flamingo and the Marquee were now rock venues. I was making a living but I thought if I didn't grab this opportunity to go to Bermuda, I would never have the chance again. What harm could six months well-paid work in the sun do? Johnny must have thought the same for we both said yes.

Bermuda is one of the most beautiful islands in the world with its pink beaches and luscious scenery. The Princess Hotel was the epitome of luxury and for the initial six months we actually lived there. After the six month period, when we decided to stay on, I moved into a house of my own and I was aghast at the cockroaches and demanded to be put back into the hotel or I would be on the next flight home. I do love the heat but not the creepy crawlies that go with it. The cockroaches would get absolutely everywhere and I remember swiping one off Johnny Butts' head during a per-formance.

In Bermuda you are not allowed to drive a car until you have lived on the island for six months, so for the first few months I rode about on a mobilette, a vehicle halfway between a motor bike and a golf buggy. This was a daring adventure for me and I careered about all over the place until one day my progress was stopped by a seawall, which I hit with great force. Luckily I was with a friend who was a doctor and he took care of me, but I still have the scars on my leg. As soon as the six months were up I bought myself a Mini.

At Christmas I flew home to see my parents and I had not been there very long when I received an urgent phone call telling me that Johnny Butts had been involved in an accident. Johnny had stayed with the Mobilette and he had hit a telegraph pole and was in a coma. I spoke to Joe Wylie daily to check on Johnny's condition but it was a hopeless situation. On 30th December I heard that he had died, aged only twenty-six. Tubby Hayes dedicated a tune to him called 'Dear Johnny B'.

I was devastated by Johnny's death but had to pull myself together enough to help the family make the arrangements to fly his body home. He was buried near Slough and many musicians clubbed together to buy a headstone of black marble with the drum kit etched on it.

With Johnny gone we had to find a replacement drummer and Joe Wylie asked me and Kenny Harris to see who we could come up with. We decided on our friend Allan Ganley and talked him into coming out there. Like me, Allan had no ties and he had no regular group of his own, so in February 1967 he flew out to Bermuda. He ended up staying there for ten years. He met and married June out there and they had a daughter Allison, who is a goddaughter for me and Kenny Harris. He also won a scholarship to Berklee School of Music in the United States and Joe let him off for a few months to take the course. As a result Allan started concentrating on his arranging and on playing the vibes.

The jazz scene on the island was non-existent but Allan and I would put together groups for infrequent broadcasts on ZBM Radio where Kenny Harris worked, often displaying Allan's arrangements. Together we would sit on the beach and wonder at how far music had taken us from our humble beginnings. But we both began to feel that the ease of life in Bermuda was making us musically a bit lazy. Often we would only play for fifteen minutes in an evening. Allan's Berklee scholarship solved the problem for him and to stretch myself I began to concentrate on the flute, knowing that if I did decide to return to London and wanted to get into the session scene, this double would be very important. I used the instrument mainly for bossa nova numbers – a music that Allan and I both love and which was ideally suited to the softer sound of the flute.

It was not all paradise in Bermuda as at that time there was some political unrest and the authorities imposed a curfew. Being a nightworker and a founder member of their musicians' union, I was one of the privileged few allowed to break the curfew. It didn't affect the tourists, who mainly stayed in their hotels at nights. Come to think of it, they spent most of the day there too, sunning themselves. I remember the film star and singer Anna Maria Alberghetti lying prone on a bed of silver foil while she went the colour of a chestnut. When she stood next to the bass you could hardly pick her out.

There was a big vogue at the time for Italian singers and many of them came to Bermuda and were extremely popular. Not my choice of music but they were nice people. One was Emilio Pericoli, who had a huge hit with a film theme song called 'Al Di La'. Around twenty years later my wife Helen and I were on holiday in Italy when we saw a poster advertising an appearance by Emilio at a nearby town. We determined to go and see him – me because of Bermuda and Helen because she had bought his records in the past. We reached the club and noticed it was full of the most elegant-ly dressed couples; we waited until Emilio drove up and I approached him. At first he stepped back in surprise at being addressed in English but then there was a roar and I was enveloped in a huge bear hug – I almost disappeared from view. We were ushered to a table, a bottle of good champagne quickly appeared and Emilio went on and began to sing the romantic Italian songs he was famous for. He stopped after a few numbers and began to talk. Helen, who understands Italian, told me he was saying how surprised he'd been that evening to be greeted by the so famous English musician with whom he'd worked at the Princess Hotel in Bermuda. The spotlight was on me and I had to stand up and take a bow whilst this classy looking audi-ence stood and cheered! The manager of the club drove us back to our hotel and we went to bed and talked about this amazing reception for hours. But it didn't end there.

The next day, our last one, we were on the beach when we heard the name Ash being paged over the loudspeakers. I immediately panicked and thought someone had died at home, but it was Emilio and he insisted on coming to take us out. He took us to his beautiful villa and showed us his vine-yards and gave us some bottles of his own wine. He had a restaurant in the basement, which is not unusual in Italy apparently. They have private restaurants to which people come by invitation only. They pay but somehow this escapes the tax authorities.

Emilio took us to a public restaurant way out in the country and we ate. Oh, did we eat! I think we counted seven different kinds of pasta, meat, chicken, fish; it kept coming. The owner was very loud, kept beaming at us and slapping us on the back, and when other people tried to enter the restaurant he drove them away! Stuffed, we couldn't manage dessert but he packed huge boxes of cakes and biscuits for us to take home. What an ending to a holiday!

We kept in touch after that and a couple of years later Emilio phoned and said he had obtained planning permission to build a small house in his vineyard. He wanted a friend to live in it and were we interested? We were at first, but when we realised how cold it got in that part of Italy in the winter and that we'd only be able to go in the short summer period, we decided against it. We did finally buy a small place in the south of France, in the Var, which we enjoyed for ten years.

Another person who became a great friend in Bermuda during the time I worked there was an Italian/Brazilian entertainer called Nelson Sardelli. He was tall, very good-looking and one of the funniest men I'd seen, on and off-stage. We became close friends and have been ever since. After I moved back from Bermuda he came to stay with me in my flat in Maida Vale and was taken with my cat Sadie and a rubber mouse she used to play with, so when Nelson left I hid the mouse in his suitcase. Some months later the mouse arrived back, mailed from Canada. I asked a friend going to Israel to send it to Nelson from there and this continued for years. The mouse went back and forth across the Atlantic, always by unusual means. Once it arrived in a box of pasta addressed to Mr Rod Ent. One time I was playing a gig in Gray's Inn for a bunch of lawyers and when I returned to my table and there was the mouse. Nelson had met a British musician on a cruise ship and, discovering that the musician knew me, Nelson asked him to take the mouse and get it to me somehow. Friends of his were playing with me that night and hence the mouse came back. Sadly, it is now lost somewhere in Las Vegas. I recommended Nelson for the Talk of the Town nightclub in London and he was so successful that his engagement was extended. He also came over here in the eighties and did a very funny spot on *The Des O'Connor Show*. Nowadays he sends me very funny emails.

I had wonderful times in Bermuda and made some good friends but I began to realise that I wanted to play something more challenging so I decided to return to England. I knew it would not be good for me to stay in Bermuda for the rest of my life so in March 1969 I came home. For me, Bermuda will always stand out as a unique and wonderful experience. Helen and I returned there in 2005 and found the island as beautiful as ever, the only difference being the vast increase in traffic. I met up with many of my old friends then and we were treated like visiting royalty. We stayed with Bill Mulder, who had been one of the managers of the Princess Hotel where I worked, and his wife Shirley. Bill is now the Dutch Consul and seems to know everyone on the island and they know him.

When I returned to England in 1969 I found things had changed. Whereas in the mid-fifties I could make a living from jazz alone, I now found I couldn't. The session scene too was beginning to shrink with the advent of synthesisers, and smaller bands were being used in recording and TV studios. So I had to phone around quite a few contractors (we call them fixers) to let them know I was back and willing to work. I did re-establish myself in the session world but never in that top layer with musicians such as Roy Willox and Bill Skeat. I didn't really want to work at that level anyway because they practically lived in the studios, whereas I wanted time to do jazz gigs, tours and other work.

Around that time in London the Grosvenor House Hotel decided to showcase jazz for a trial period and Ronnie Scott formed a big band to accompany Ella Fitzgerald. The support group for this splendid offering was the Oscar Peterson Trio. I was delighted to be a part of this very high profile gig.

Not long after, the pianist Phil Phillips asked me if I would be interested in joining his quartet, which was resident at the Talk of the Town. Saxophonist Alan Skidmore was leaving and I would be his replacement. Phil told me I would be free to put in a dep if I got a tour or wanted to do something else, so I accepted. This was a wonderful position to be in and it left me free to do the many, many tours that came my way shortly after I joined Phil.

The group simply had to go on and play for the first fifteen minutes and later do a couple of dance sets of the same length. It was all standard tunes and the odd pop song, after which came the main acts, accompanied by a big band conducted by Burt Rhodes. The Talk was a big Las Vegas-style nightclub operation with a cabaret and live girlie show and it attracted some wonderful guests. One of them was Matt Monro who by 1970 had become a huge star. Whenever he played the Talk he would ask for me to be added to the resident big band. So that meant a quick dash between playing in the small group on tenor to play second alto in the big band. I was happy to do it and to know that fame had not changed Matt from the unassuming guy he was when we had first met in Cardiff. I wound up staying seven years at the Talk and thoroughly enjoyed them.

11

Sinatra

They say life begins at forty. As I reached that milestone my career certainly began a new phase. My earlier breaks with Kenny Baker and Ray Charles had come with a phone call and my next was no exception. Out of the blue in the spring of 1970 I received a call from John Flanagan, a fixer. John had been a drummer back when I first started and had also taught me how to drive. He had since turned to contracting and this is how the phone call went:

'Here Vic, Harold Davison is bringing Frank Sinatra over in May and he wants some woodwind players. Do you fancy it?'

'*What* did you say?' I replied, as he sounded so down to earth.

'D'you fancy doing it, Vic?'

Fancy doing it! Sinatra! Yes! Yes! I was exhilarated, I was shaking, I couldn't believe it.

I had been a fan of Sinatra from way back in the forties. I'd bought his albums, followed his career and seen his movies. I put him on a pedestal along with Astaire, Parker and Getz. He had transformed popular singing from its often stiff artifice of the interwar years into something that was highly expressive and a true art form. His phrasing, his feel and the material he used attracted musicians as much as the general public. Allan Ganley and I would often sit and marvel at the wonderful arrangements done by such masters as Nelson Riddle, Don Costa and Billy May, who always seemed to produce that something extra for him.

I had first seen Sinatra perform soon after I turned professional in 1950 when he came to England to do some dates with Billy Ternent's band, which was not at all a suitable choice to accompany him. This was not a good time for Sinatra; he was locked into a dissatisfying contract with Columbia Records, his marriage was on the rocks and he had suffered a complete loss of voice at one performance. The general opinion was that he was finished – but that was before *From Here to Eternity*, the film for which he won a well-deserved Oscar, and the fabulous series of recordings he went on to make with Capitol Records. During Sinatra's 1950 London visit I went to the Trocadero at Elephant and Castle to see the show and, amazing to recall, I was able to move twenty or so rows forward in the nearly empty hall. Frank looked a bit jaded but he was still singing brilliantly despite the fact that he and Billy Ternent just did not hit it off. They kept disagreeing over one thing and another and in one exchange Frank came out with: 'Next time I come over I'll bring Borrah Minevitch's Harmonica Rascals.' Things did not improve and much the same thing happened when I saw them at the Commodore at Hammersmith a few days later.

In 1962 Sinatra came over to do a concert at the Royal Festival Hall with a sextet of Bill Miller, Harry Klee, Ralph Pena, Emil Richards, Al Viola and Irv Cottler. The event was part of a worldwide charity tour and this, his only London date, was compered by David Jacobs. I was in John Dankworth's band at the time and was overjoyed when we were booked to play the first half of the bill, along with Cleo Laine. As soon as the band finished its spot, I scuttled off to my seat in the third row of the stalls to gaze at Frank.

My first engagement with Sinatra was in 1970 and came about under somewhat peculiar circumstances. He was appearing with the Count Basie band at the Royal Festival Hall but had reservations about their woodwind doubling. He had a valid point as the driving swing for which the Basie band was famous seldom made use of clarinets and bass clarinets. But he was keen not to upset Basie. So John Flanagan booked Roy Willox, Dougie Robinson, Ray Swinfield, Duncan Lamont and me and, in order not to hurt any feelings, the Basie band was told we were from a symphony orchestra. This was a dream assignment. We were in the best seats in the house and only had to pick up our flutes and clarinets for about half a dozen numbers, such as 'My Way' and 'Strangers in the Night'. The rest of the time we were listening to the band and Sinatra, and it was pure magic.

Later that year Sinatra came over for a star-studded charity event and this time he asked for a full British orchestra. I was again asked for, and some of the country's top musicians were in the orchestra: Don Lusher, Kenny Baker, Ronnie Ross and Ronnie Chamberlain were just some of them. Generally speaking, musicians did not rate vocalists very highly at that time, thinking they got in the way of the more talented instrumentalists, but Sinatra had the power to move every one of those seasoned professionals. He addressed the musicians directly, rather than going through a musical director, and was extremely clear in his instructions, especially those regarding dynamics. Accompanying a vocalist is an art form that relies entirely on the orchestra being willing to subjugate itself to the singer. British bands had sometimes seemed woefully ignorant of this and now came the acid test. Things went smoothly, although Sinatra would think nothing of stopping a piece midway if he considered something was not quite right and that his lyrics might not be heard.

He also displayed a familiarity with every nuance of the arrangements, something that I encountered while rehearsing 'A Very Good Year', with its distinctive link passages between choruses which I played on clarinet. I felt very exposed as I stood there and each time I was interrupted by Sinatra declaring, 'That should be an oboe.' The conductor, Don Costa, motioned for me to continue but each time the link occurred Sinatra would do the same thing: 'Should be an oboe!'

My heart was pounding and when there was a break in the rehearsal I went over to Sinatra, who was leafing through music at the piano, feeling I had to explain that there was no oboist in the orchestra. I hesitatingly told him that we could bring in an oboe player if he wanted one but Sinatra, looking puzzled at first, said, 'No, it's fine. It sounded beautiful with the clarinet – leave it in.' My legs had turned to jelly as I walked back to my seat. Whew! I guess he was just so used to the sound of the oboe playing that passage that anything else must have seemed a little odd at first.

Besides Frank, the concert included Bob Hope, Grace Kelly and Lord Louis Mountbatten, who was compering in place of Noel Coward who was ill. While we rehearsed during the afternoon we suddenly heard an off-key version of 'Strangers in the Night' being sung off stage and as we all looked up Bob Hope strolled on. Frank burst into laughter and, much to the delight of Bob Hope, sailed into 'Thanks for the Memory' and the two of them kidded around. While we were watching this impromptu cabaret I noticed a rather plain middle-aged lady sitting in the stalls gazing at all this rather intently. I was astounded, when she came on to introduce the show that night, to see that she had metamorphosed into the beautiful, glamorous Grace Kelly.

With the orchestra – which always contained the very best of British musicians – we travelled all over Europe and the Middle East as well as England. We did a tour approximately every eighteen months until Sinatra retired in 1992. We played a different city in Europe every two days, many of them in Germany which seemed to have more large cities than anywhere else. I saw places I never thought I'd see and it was all paid for, with top class hotels everywhere we went. But, truthfully, I would have paid my own way just to have the thrill of working with Sinatra.

Everyone – including all those hardened musicians who had been in the business a long time and done all sorts of work with different artists in studios and clubs and concerts – was very impressed to be working with Frank. I would not say anyone was scared of him but he was so thorough that it could make you feel slightly edgy. His instructions were always definite, he knew what he wanted and it was impossible not to respect his artistry and dedication. Artists like Tony Bennett and Mel Tormé and, in Britain, Cleo Laine command your respect because they think like musicians. Sinatra was possibly the first of the modern singers to think that way.

People have said to me: 'Surely, when you played for Frank Sinatra, being so familiar with his music, you didn't have to read anything.' It wasn't quite like that. Knowing it from a record is different from playing it for real, although I must admit it helps with the phrasing. But you still have to read the notes. Being in the midst of all that unforgettable music, playing all those wonderful charts, seeing the glow on the faces of the audience, was probably the highlight of my musical life.

I got to know some of Frank's regular musicians that he would bring over for the tours, like Bill Miller his pianist and Irv Cottler the drummer. Irv had a wonderful strong sound and you could always hear him driving the band. He and I became very friendly and always made a point of meeting up for breakfast on tour. Sadly, Irv died just after one of the tours and it was a great loss.

I have been asked many times if I got to know Sinatra at all. I cannot say I did. He was always polite and friendly and would say, 'Hi fellas,' when he arrived and then come over to the saxes and ask, 'How's Robert Farnon?' He did this every time because Robert had arranged and conducted Frank's 1962 album *Great Songs from Great Britain*. Frank was so much a star that not one of us would have had the temerity to go over and start chatting to him; it was like being in the presence of royalty. He would drop in to some of the end-of-tour parties organised for the band by his son Frank Sinatra Jr, often in the company of Roger Moore and Gregory Peck, two of his close friends. His friends and admirers included celebrities of all kinds. At one show, I rushed into the men's room some five minutes before the start and was a little uncomfortable to find an impressively built man standing rather too close to me. I then noticed that standing alongside me was our Prime Minister, John Major, who left with his bodyguard at the same time as I did.

Back in the early seventies we would do about four or five rehearsals for each tour – always in London – at the Savoy Hotel, at Henry Wood Hall in the East End and often at the Sheraton Hotel in Knightsbridge, where the few musicians that Frank brought with him from the States would be staying.

Frank himself would rent the whole second floor of the Savoy Hotel for the duration of his stay for himself and his entourage. All rooms had to be left unlocked at all times in case Frank felt ready to party. If Frank was in the mood to party he wasn't prepared to knock on doors – he would just walk in and demand the presence of whoever was sleeping in there. In later years, wherever we played, he would have a plane to fly him direct to Geneva for the night as, by this stage of his life, he preferred to sleep always in the same place and Geneva was pretty central from anywhere in Europe.

Frank would be very meticulous at these rehearsals. More often than not he'd say, 'Too loud,' and he was always right. Except for charts where we needed to really blow loud he liked us to play at a nice low level. We were, after all, backing a vocalist and not trying to drown him out. At one concert in Amsterdam he asked for all the musicians' microphones to be turned off. He was right – the orchestra sounded perfect that way.

Sinatra changed his musical directors several times over the twenty-two years I worked with him. First it was Bill Miller, who didn't want the responsibility of being musical director and having to coordinate all the other players. He just wanted to drift on and play his own part sitting at the piano accompanying Frank and then go home without worrying about anything to do with the show. He was responsible for the famous introduction to 'One for my Baby', which, sung by Sinatra, became the definitive version of this Arlen-Mercer standard. Eventually, Frank Sinatra Jr became musical director and I recall one rehearsal for a televised concert in Milan when Frank Jr himself decided to sing. Frank Sr had stopped coming to rehearsals by this time. He knew exactly what he was going to be doing so he would leave the rehearsals to his MD. His son had had a career as a singer but he was fated always to be known as 'son of' rather than as a performer in his own right; it must have been impossible to follow in the footsteps of such a giant. At concerts we would play the same twenty or thirty tunes – the big hits plus songs from his albums – but for this rehearsal we went through the whole Sinatra book, which included hundreds of arrangements. He was obviously indulging himself but he knew his father's arrangements backwards. At times he sounded uncannily like him and we had a marvellous few hours.

Frank Jr was one of the chaps. On the road he could easily have travelled with his father in private jets and stayed in luxurious hotels but he chose to be with us musicians, riding on buses and staying in the same hotels as we did. One time in Italy, the only hotel within reach of the venue was a very modest one with small boxy rooms and a tiny bathroom in which you could shower as you sat on the toilet! That night there was a storm and the power failed. With it went the water supply. Frank Jr came round to all of us with Coca Cola to clean our teeth and he was down on his hands and knees trying to figure out how to get the power back on. He is a very pleasant down-to-earth man and also a great film buff and on these tours we would have long conversations about our favourite actors. He told me his father's favourite was

Bela Lugosi. As Count Dracula, of course, he had a motive entirely different from Frank's each time he opened his mouth!

Frank Jr threw two great parties for us, in Dublin and in Athens. At one of them I was asked to make a speech on behalf of the band. There had been a mix-up at the airport and as a result some of the musicians flew club class and some flew economy and it had all got rather heated; so I began my speech by singing, 'Come fly with me, let's fly economy.' Luckily Frank Sr did not come in until a moment after I had sat down.

In 1979 we did a concert at the site of the Pyramids in Egypt. A stage had been set up and out front were tables gleaming with white tablecloths and shining silver cutlery. The dinner and show were in aid of the special charity of Mrs Anwar Sadat, the Egyptian President's wife, and tickets for this event cost fourteen thousand dollars each. One would have expected that our audience would have consisted of wealthy Arab sheikhs but it was mostly Texan oil millionaires who had flown over just to catch the show. We rehearsed in the afternoon in unbearable heat. After two numbers, Frank, who was wearing a white denim suit, stopped us and said, 'Guys, forget the rehearsal. Most of you have done the show already so we'll do it cold tonight.' Much relieved, we began to retire to the shade and he called out, 'Put your instruments away or they'll melt.' I have worked with lesser artists who would not have shown such thoughtfulness towards their fellow performers.

You can imagine the scene by the time it was evening. The atmosphere was already electric because, with the orchestra assembled on stage, there was a *Son et Lumière* in which a voice that sounded like Richard Burton's narrated the story of ancient Egypt and the Pyramids. The orchestra then played for dinner. Finally, through the desert past the illuminated Sphinx and the Pyramids came a cavalcade of cars with blazing sirens. A limousine pulled up directly in front of the stage and out stepped Sinatra who went right into his first number. It was magical. Here you had the Pyramids, one of the Eight Wonders of the World, and Sinatra, who I would call the Ninth Wonder. Part of the concert was filmed for the television news.

Although I am sorry to say I never recorded with Sinatra, I did do a few television shows with him when he flew to Milan or Madrid to record them. I also did some television shows with him in Ireland. Many of these shows – including the 1970 one with Grace Kelly – are now available on video and DVD, and if you look at the images you can often see me sitting just behind Frank.

Sinatra appealed to all audiences – he got as much applause in Iran as he did in Israel and they loved him as much in Ireland as they did in England.

The Irish audiences were the only ones that joined in with him on all the popular numbers – he was really taken aback at first but then relaxed and went with it. During 'My Way' the whole audience were singing along, waving sparklers back and forth. It was the first time I had seen this, although nowadays it is quite common at concerts with pop musicians. I have played Ireland many times in the course of my career and always had a great welcome. One of my cousins is a professor at Trinity College Dublin and, after a gap of forty-five years, I managed to catch up with him on one of the Sinatra gigs.

The Irish are so 'Irish' that at times I wonder if they are doing it purposely. I was in a pub there recently and one of my pals asked for a port and brandy. The barman looked at him speculatively and enquired, '... and would that be a brandy and port?' Allan Ganley was on holiday in Ireland a few years ago and went to buy a newspaper. 'Would ye be wanting today's paper or yesterday's?' the vendor asked. 'Today's,' said Allan. 'Ah well, ye'll have to come back tomorrow for that.'

Sinatra played Iran during the seventies doing a couple of concerts for the Shah, just before the Ayatollah took over. We did one public concert and also one just for the Shah and his wealthy friends. From there we went straight to Israel to do a couple of concerts in Jerusalem. For the events in Israel we were told that a very fine Israeli string session would be playing as part of our orchestra. But there had been a big misunderstanding between the agents because we discovered that the the musicians were students, all from different countries, studying at the university there. I have to say that they were quite unsuitable for our kind of music but Frank showed the same wonderful adaptability that he had in the past and understood and accepted the situation.

We did many concerts in Italy, where the audiences thought of Sinatra as one of their own, even though he hardly knew a word of Italian. I was always mystified by Italian audiences. They always arrived very late and would walk around during the performance, eating and drinking. During the first half of the concert, before Frank came on, there would hardly be anyone in the audience. This happened in Pompeii, where we played in the ruined amphitheatre. The first half featured singers Steve Lawrence and Eydie Gormé and the theatre was empty. So my wife Helen went to sit out front to watch them, knowing the show was a sell-out and she would have to move for the second half. She was chatting to one of the sound men and was oblivious of the fact that the theatre was filling up for the Sinatra part of the show. Suddenly she spotted me with the rest of the orchestra on stage and looked around in surprise to find that nobody had asked her to move. The tickets were extremely expensive and much in demand and where the people who had bought the tickets ended up we have never found out. Helen got to see the show in comfort, waving at me between numbers.

Pompeii was incredibly hot and humid and Frank Jr was busy bustling around spraying everyone's ankles with mosquito repellent. Frank Sr's dressing room was no more than a wooden shack but there was not a word of complaint. We were very moved by the humility of the man when Frank walked by with his manager, all excited, and said 'D'you know what just happened? The Chief of Police brought me in – and he asked me for my autograph. How about that? The Chief of Police wanted *my* autograph!' To him, the Chief of Police was far more important than he was.

In 1980 we did two whole weeks in London – one at the Royal Festival Hall and one at the Royal Albert Hall. At the time it was unheard of to take over those two venues for a week at a time, but every concert was packed, with tickets selling for exorbitant prices on the black market. At the end of the two weeks we musicians presented Frank with a trophy. He came into our dressing room where the promoter Harold Davison had laid on a meal for everyone. The orchestra had all contributed towards the cost of the trophy to commemorate ten years of Frank's performances with a British orchestra. He was delighted. We had thought he would come in briefly, accept it, and leave but he stayed with us for over an hour. He said, 'Fire ahead with any questions.' And Don Lusher and I, and most of us, started asking him all sorts of questions about his time with the bands of Tommy Dorsey and Harry James. Don asked about his breath control and Frank told us how he used to watch Dorsey play and observe how he breathed and he had learned a lot from that.

Having played for him for over twenty years I did hear changes in his voice over time. On the last two or three tours it got a bit tired. The charisma was always there but his breath control, for which he had always been known, was not too reliable. However, he was well into his seventies by then and for such a vocalist he had a career which lasted longer than most. A couple of the arrangements were altered over the years to accommodate the changes in his voice but most of them remained in the same pitch.

The press had an almost obsessive interest in Sinatra's private life and saw us musicians, who worked closely with him, as a way to getting a scoop. Some reporters who phoned me were genuinely trying to get my feelings at working with such a superstar but others were only looking for gossip. A journalist from the *Daily Express* was on the phone to me for ages insisting that I should say Frank's voice had gone, so she could quote me. When I refused to say anything other than that I still felt it a great honour to work with him, her article concentrated on his weight and his hair.

The press have always been ready to bring Sinatra down. He never had time for them after he found out they were only interested in his private life and not his music. They printed many things which were completely untrue. I do not intend to go into the rumours about his links with the Mafia but I will say that as an Italian-American he would have gone to school with many of the Mafia faces and at that time nearly any venue worth appearing in would have been controlled by the Mafia. So he could hardly have avoided knowing them. Had the press concentrated on his artistry instead of his wives and so-called Mafia dealings, he would have been far more approachable and willing to give interviews. On one occasion I was outraged to see a picture of Frank in a newspaper singing in an empty auditorium in Germany with a caption indicating that Frank was a has-been and could not attract an audience. I was there at the time and know that the picture was taken at a rehearsal.

Sinatra always drew a full house and gave a great show. One of the greatest, in the 1980s, was called *The Ultimate Event*. This was a tremendous bill featuring not only Frank himself but also Liza Minnelli and Sammy Davis Jr. The three of them knew each other very well and the atmosphere between them was as if three friends were simply enjoying being together. We did not know it but Sammy was nearing the end of his life then. At the beginning of the tour he was always seeking us out, swapping jokes and generally being one of the guys, but towards the end he began to look haggard and would stay alone in a corner. He tried to be his old lively self but he knew, I'm sure, that his light was beginning to dim. He was always very considerate and natural and an enormous talent. When the three singers joined together at the end of the show and did a medley of their hits it was one of those times when you feel incredibly happy but also very emotional at the same time.

Of all the things I've done in my career, probably the highlight for me was working with Frank Sinatra. I consider myself a jazz musician, and sometimes a session musician, and doing the Sinatra show was almost like doing a jazz gig because of the superb arrangements and his wonderful phrasing. To sit in the middle of that fabulous orchestra and hear that sensational music going on all around me was just the best thing that could happen. I was very fortunate. To me, playing with Sinatra was a great honour and an incredibly happy experience.

12

Other Americans – Stars and Shows

For me, the 1970s were incredibly busy with a perpetual round of tours with American entertainers and recording work, mostly of a commercial nature. Commercial work was financially rewarding and was very welcome at a time when jazz soloists were struggling to exist on improvised music alone. I had anticipated this situation while I was in Bermuda and perhaps was better prepared than some of my colleagues. Going to the recording studios for all manner of jingles, albums and movies acquired the regularity of going to the office and I found myself recording with a wide range of artists. This could have proved to be a tiresome way to financial gain were it not for the fact that it also provided me with the chance to work with truly great talents.

In 1970 I was booked for a date at Abbey Road Studios with Quincy Jones. Quincy had written wonderful arrangements for Basie, Sinatra and many others and had a great career as a producer, talent scout and film score composer as well as having made many big band jazz albums. I was a long-time fan of his writing and eagerly anticipated the session.

Abbey Road had been made into a household name by the Beatles and after they broke up and pursued independent careers they still used the studios. I was booked for a studio date with Ringo Starr, making an album of standard songs entitled *Sentimental Journey*. He had lined up, besides Quincy, such big-name composers and arrangers as Leonard Bernstein, Oliver Nelson, John Dankworth and George Martin. All this was unknown to me. I arrived expecting a roaring big band date and brought everything with me from saxes to piccolos, but as soon as Quincy and Ringo arrived I could see the session would be far less taxing. In fact all I had to do was play alto flute behind Ringo's vocal of Quincy's arrangement of 'Love is a Many Splendoured Thing'. To make it easier for Ringo, Quincy had written a very simple chart with just long notes. I am glad that I recorded with Quincy, even though it was not at all what I expected.

Later the same year I did a couple of weeks with Marlene Dietrich. I was playing alto for this and sat alongside the marvellous saxophonist Peter King, who was also temporarily forsaking jazz to accompany world class entertainers. Marlene looked wonderful on stage. Although she must have been around seventy then she looked no older than forty. She would take hours to get ready and would always wear the same tight, figure-hugging, sequinned dress. One night some time before show time I went past Marlene's dressing room and caught sight of what I thought was a dresser, an old lady doing some stitching to the sequinned gown, but upon looking again I saw it was Marlene looking totally unrecognisable off-stage. It was remarkable how this gaunt old woman could transform herself into the youthful glamorous siren of her stage act.

An excellent singer I worked with was Jack Jones, who had a library of great arrangements, many of them written by Pat Williams. Jack's father, Allan, often accompanied him on these tours; he had been a heartthrob himself many years before, playing the romantic lead in the 1937 classic Marx Brothers movie *A Day at the Races* and introducing 'Donkey Serenade' in the movie *The Firefly*. Allan was a very sweet man, very proud of his son's achievements. Jack too was proud of his success and one night he decided to reward the band for its support by showing them a hard porn video (*Deep Throat*) in his hotel room. To our astonishment he had taken off the usual sighs, groans and grunts and replaced them with a soundtrack of his own voice singing his hits.

Most of the vocalists I worked with sang standards but I also played with some pop artists. One of the most financially rewarding weeks was when I worked with the Carpenters. For this date at the London Palladium a special scaffold had been erected on the stage and each musician was seated by himself on his own piece of the scaffold. Every concert was recorded and later an album was issued. The concerts were a great success and, although they were huge stars at the time, both Karen and Richard seemed unaffected and simply got on with the job.

I also worked at the Palladium with Anne Murray, the Canadian singer who had a big hit with 'Snowbird'. I was seated at the side of the stage and had to start the show with a solo piccolo part. As I raised it to my lips the chair keeled over and down I went off the stage and out of sight. I hurt my shoulder badly but was able to finish the concert. I was due back at the Palladium the following day to do a date with Liberace and, although I managed the rehearsal and the first show, I had to give up the rest of the week as I was in agony.

Although it was fun, and lucrative, to work with pop artists, my love was still for standard songs and I was lucky in being able to work with some of the finest standard singers ever. After Sinatra I would pick out Lena Horne, Mel Tormé and Tony Bennett. They are singers of real quality – in their voices, the songs they sing, the arrangements they use and their whole approach. Peggy Lee too is in that league and Sinatra conducted an album for her, *The Man I Love*, back in the Capitol era of the fifties.

I first worked with Lena Horne and Tony Bennett on the same package but I have since worked with Tony several times on his own. He is a real jazz fan and he sang the works of such great arrangers as Torrie Zito and Al Cohn so I usually had lots of tenor sax solos to play. I am really delighted that Tony has an ongoing appeal and has made such an impression on the young people of today. They seem to love his interpretation of good standards and he doesn't change his style to accommodate them. I worked with Tony some years ago on a Chris Evans *TFI Friday* television show with the BBC Big Band. We did a couple of numbers and were astounded that the audience of youngsters, the rock and pop generation, were going crazy over him – a man in his seventies singing songs of yesteryear.

Another constant with Tony over many years was his piano player Ralph Sharon. Ralph and I knew each other back in the fifties when he was doing jazz dates in London before moving to America. Back then Harry Klein and I worked together so much that people occasionally used to get us mixed up. When I did the *TFI* programme I hadn't seen Ralph in years so I said, 'Hi Ralph,' and he looked up and said, 'Hey Harry!' It was all quickly sorted out and the last time I saw Ralph he quickly said, 'Hello *Vic*!' That was at the Royal Albert Hall in 1999 for which Tony, who usually works with just a rhythm section, had added a full orchestra for two concerts. Ralph took Helen and me to meet Tony and we had a long chat in his dressing room. Tony was simply charming and we had our pictures taken with him as we talked over concerts we had done over the years.

Whilst busy with television and session work I still was able to find the time to tour with visiting American artists. One remarkable tour was with Liza Minnelli. Most of the tours I had done included dates in England, usually London, but this one was entirely located on the Continent, and the promoter was Danish. We travelled around Europe in style in a private plane and were treated like royalty with the best hotels, the best everything. One night, many of us in the band wound up in a rather shady nightclub in Hamburg and to our surprise Liza appeared with her party. This was the last place we expected to see a big star like Liza Minnelli but she was always down to earth and friendly. When we came to leave, we found that she had picked up the tab.

She was very approachable and I felt I had to tell her how one number she did in her show affected me. She has a song in her act that is dedicated to deaf people, during which she would use sign language while she sang. Because of my parents, this moved me tremendously and one night I went to her dressing room and told her how deeply I felt about it. She was very sympathetic and touched by that.

When I played the London Palladium in 1986 with Liza, I felt ill during the concert and went home to bed wondering if I was coming down with something. I awoke suddenly at five o'clock the next morning and told Helen, 'I don't feel well.' She could tell by the tone of my voice that something was really wrong and immediately began phoning for a doctor. Before she had completed dialling I fell back on the bed and from out of my mouth came a veritable fountain of blood, drenching the bed, the carpet, the walls and Helen herself. She was horrified and was screaming, 'No, no!' but, on automatic pilot, she switched her dialling from the doctor to 999. The ambulance came very quickly and rushed me to the Royal Free Hospital where I received more than five pints of blood. The doctors told me that my oesophagus had become inflamed over a period of time and had begun to bleed slowly into my stomach until I could take no more and up it came. Strangely, I felt very euphoric after losing all that blood and I was walking about saying I felt fine. I've since been told that with a large blood loss you get a 'high'. This illness, I felt sure, would mean the end of the Liza Minnelli week but I was wrong – the worst was over and I recovered quickly. As it was a Saturday I missed only one show.

Liza Minnelli is one of the stars who still insist on a full orchestra for their tours, as did Sinatra. Johnny Mathis was another. Johnny is a very pleasant guy, quiet and reserved, who liked to play golf with any of the musicians who knew how. From the eighties onwards, so many cuts were made to the costs of tours that very few of the artists used a full band anymore. It's just more economical to use a rhythm section and a couple of blowers. These days technology can make 'live' musicians redundant but it cannot replace the atmosphere that a full band can provide. Another artist who insisted on a real orchestra was Barbra Streisand, and she is one of the very few that I haven't worked with. I have long been a fan of hers, since the days when she sang standards with great arrangements by guys like Peter Matz. I did a movie with him, *Stepping Out*, a few years back.

The first time Shirley MacLaine came over was to do a week at the Palladium. Most people just thought of her as a great actress, which of course she is, with a string of great movies to her credit, especially *The Apartment* and *Some Came Running*, but her act showed all her talents. She sang, danced, did comedy, the whole bit, and it caused a sensation, so much so that it made the national press headlines the next day. All the musicians loved being part of the orchestra for this show and when it was extended we all got out of any prior commitments in order to stay with the fun. We later did six days in Paris with her.

For some reason or other we got to Paris with just a short while to go before the show started. I hadn't eaten and the quickest solution was a hamburger on the hotel terrace. However, when I opened up a bottle of ketchup it exploded – all over the clothes I was to wear for the concert! Luckily the show was being held in the hotel where I was eating and my clothes were whipped away, cleaned and pressed and returned to my room in what seemed like minutes. I was able to go to the concert with a freshly laundered, pressed dinner suit but since that day I have *never* opened a bottle that has been sitting out in the sun.

One of Shirley's tours was organised by a very tight-fisted promoter who did everything he could to save money. When the band arrived in Brussels we found we had been booked into a really disgusting place but when we complained the promoter simply shrugged us off. At that time the fixer used to put me in charge of the band (as he was unable to travel everywhere with us) so, feeling very angry, I said, 'OK guys – out!' We hailed some taxis and went to the hotel where Shirley was staying and I marched up to reception and told them we were Shirley's musicians and needed rooms. They were rather flustered but found rooms for us and we heard no more from our dubious promoter. But the whole episode left us with a bad feeling about the tour.

Shirley herself wasn't too forthcoming with us – in fact she could be very aloof. As she entered for a rehearsal she would say, 'Hi, guys.' But that was about it and on the last tour or two she said nothing. She wasn't exactly unfriendly but she was indifferent and this annoyed quite a few of us, most of whom had played for Sinatra who would always say a few words. We felt she did not value our contribution and we mentioned our feelings one day in Vienna to her manager, saying that at the sound check earlier that day she hadn't even acknowledged us. He obviously had a word with her because the next night she came running over to the band with a, 'Hiya, Fellas! How you doing? Great!'

I have to say that the nicest person among the big stars that I ever worked with was Howard Keel. Howard had a deep and true baritone, perfect for the leads he played in so many musicals. It was not the sort of voice I personally went for, as I preferred artistes who sang in a more jazz-like style, but I had to admire its perfection. Although to me he was the star of such great movies as *Kiss me Kate*, *Annie Get your Gun* and *Seven Brides for Seven Brothers*, to the audiences he was known for his part in the television soap *Dallas* and people would call out to him, 'How's Miss Ellie?' He was always gracious and a real gentleman. Howard would introduce every member of the orchestra to the audience by name – even the deputies – and say a few words about where the musician had come from or what he had done; this took time and trouble and I don't know anyone else who would have bothered. One time Helen and I entered a restaurant in Manchester where Howard was sitting with his manager.

'Hey, come and join us!' he cried, and then, 'Oh well, I can see you two lovebirds want to be alone – we'll have a drink later.' When I asked for the bill at the end of our meal I was told that Howard had already arranged to pay it. I have nothing but fond memories of Howard.

At the end of these tours the artists would often present the band with small gifts as mementos of the tour. Shirley gave us a wallet with her image outlined in gold, Jerry Lewis presented us with a lighter with his caricature on it, Dean Martin gave us a bottle of Scotch; the only one who didn't give us anything was Sinatra, but just playing with him and that beautiful music was thanks enough. I have a book, an album and a photograph which Frank autographed for me and that is better than anything.

Around this time, jazz pianist and Musicians' Union executive Johnny Patrick used to provide a group to entertain the American Ambassador and all the top union leaders at Winfield House, the home of the American Ambassador in Regents Park. I made a complete fool of myself when the Ambassador came up, held out his hand, and said, 'Hi, I'm Charlie Price.' I thought he said Charley Pride and blurted out, 'Oh hi, we've worked together in the past.' Ambassador Price looked slightly bewildered but diplomatically nodded and passed on to the next player.

Someone who placed great importance on getting famous entertainers to reveal their private selves is Michael Parkinson. He was primarily a journalist and had come into mainstream broadcasting through an apprenticeship on regional programmes in the north of England. He has hosted several popular television chat shows including one called *Parkinson* which ran from 1971 to 1982 and he took every opportunity to speak to legends such as Orson Welles, Bing

Crosby, Bob Hope, Bette Davis and – as he had a great passion for jazz – Duke Ellington, Oscar Peterson, Buddy Rich, Ronnie Scott and Woody Herman. He also had a live quintet on the show, led by Harry Stoneham with whom I had worked on the *Sunday Break* television shows. Harry had his own group of musicians but if the saxophone player was unable to make the show because of a prior engagement, Harry asked me to come in. I remember being in the lift with Harry during the recording of my first show at BBC Television Centre at White City in London when Parkinson entered and Harry introduced me. I was astonished when his reaction was. 'Vic Ash! My goodness, I used to come and hear you play back in the fifties.' Since that time we have often met and had chats and I used to see Michael waving at me from the audience when I was doing the Sinatra concerts.

The television shows were not musically demanding, often requiring the band to play only introductory music if the guests were not singers. The shows on which the quintet performed were sometimes recorded at a little theatre in Guys Hospital (yes!) but if the artists on the show needed a big band Harry Stoneham would assemble one and, more often than not, we would record the show at BBC Television Centre. The Wednesday shows, which were only added for the last few years of the run, were done live and for the Saturday ones we would rehearse on Saturday afternoon and the show would either be pre-recorded or go out live that same evening.

The *Parkinson* shows were a joy for me, for I got to see and hear and often speak to the huge stars of film and television, writers, comedians, politicians; but while I enjoyed seeing all these celebrities the greatest thrill was the song writers.

After the show, a small nucleus of the band was invited to the hospitality suite, together with Michael Parkinson and guests from the show. We had food and drink and a chance to meet the guests. One highspot was meeting Johnny Mercer. Here was one of the most prolific lyricists of all time, who had written beautiful words to tunes by all the great composers – 'Autumn Leaves', 'Moon River', 'I Thought About You', 'Goody Goody' – the list is endless. He was happy to talk to me and he was a truly charming man answering my questions with ease and pleasure. I also met Sammy Cahn, who with Jimmy van Heusen wrote many songs for Sinatra. My favourite Cahn lyric is 'The Second Time Around'.

One guest we looked forward to was Phil Silvers. Of course, he will always be associated with Sergeant Bilko in the 1950s comedy series *Bilko* and to many jazz musicians *Bilko* was special. He had also written a lovely set of lyrics to the tune of 'Nancy with the Laughing Face'. Somehow you just don't think of these great stars getting old, you just picture them as they were, but when Phil Silvers walked in we were crushed – here was an old man. Apparently he used to play clarinet and the *Parkinson* team wanted to get him to play and asked me if Phil could blow my instrument. I was more than happy to agree but Silvers was adamant that he wanted to play a Boosey and Hawkes instrument, and not mine, which was a Buffet. The production team phoned an instrument shop, which then sent a Boosey and Hawkes clarinet to the studio in a cab. I was asked to try it first and found it was unplayable, which rather surprised me knowing who was going to play it. I said, 'I don't think you'll play this, Phil,' to which he replied offhandedly, 'I didn't want to play anyway.' It seemed that he felt he was being pushed into doing it against his will. The actual interview was also an anticlimax and Phil seemed disinterested. It wasn't funny and this was not the Bilko we knew and loved, but some comics are not funny when they're not working. It is a job and they just turn on when they are performing, I guess.

James Cagney too seemed to have metamorphosed into someone else when he appeared on *Parkinson*. He had made his name in films like *Public Enemy* and would always be associated in the public's mind with gangsters. It was a role he was still playing as late as the mid-fifties when he starred opposite Doris Day in the film *Love Me or Leave Me* playing Marty the Gimp. Cagney had another side; he had started off in vaudeville and the film *Yankee Doodle Dandy*, for which he won an Oscar, showed off his dancing skills to perfection.

Parkinson achieved a major coup when he reunited Cagney and his old friend and frequent on-screen collaborator Pat O'Brien for a joint interview. O'Brien's friendship with Cagney went back to the twenties when both were working their apprenticeships in repertory theatre companies. Fifty years on, they made a dramatic contrast: O'Brien seemed ageless, his twinkle-eyed Irish manner accompanied by an upright posture and an almost irrepressible willingness to talk. Cagney sat virtually motionless beside him in a wheelchair, a pale figure hardly recognisable as the dynamic actor of the thirties. However, for all his bounce and youthfulness, it wasn't O'Brien who mesmerised the audience or raised the best laughs.

Cagney made the whole studio laugh when he recalled being accosted by a small child shortly after the release of *Angels with Dirty Faces*. This 1938 film was about an idolised villain, played by Cagney, who acts like a coward when finally confronted with the electric chair in order to destroy the myth that surrounds him and not corrupt the morals of his young followers. Cagney told the audience how the child eyed him up and down slyly for several minutes before enquiring, 'Did ya or didn't ya?' Baffled, Cagney asked the child what he meant only to get the same question. 'Did I or didn't I what, son?' he asked. 'Did ya or didn't ya go yellow that time ya went to the chair,' replied the kid, clearly unable to separate the actor from his on-screen characters that were such potent images.

For me the appearances of men like Cagney and Silvers were not easily dismissed as disappointments but were more like revelations. Parkinson's interview could serve to highlight just how far some of these stars were from their golden eras and how dated some of their ideas seemed in the modern world. John Wayne, in London to shoot the movie *Brannigan*, seemed reluctant to talk about his cinematic achievements, merely answering yes or 'nope' to most questions. He preferred to divert the conversation into political waters.

One guest who surprised me was the comedian Marty Feldman. We were quite friendly in my early days as a musician and used to travel together on the tube. While talking to Parkinson he pointed to me in the orchestra and said, 'Look, the Jewish Charlie Parker!' (I wish). He then told Parkinson that I had lent him a book, *Crazy like a Fox* by S. J. Perelman, which had encouraged him to become a comedian, but I can't honestly say I remember lending him this.

It was naturally the musical guests that captivated me. Bing Crosby showed on *Parkinson* that age had not affected his beautiful off-hand vocal delivery. I had toured with him sometime earlier and done a week at the Palladium in London with him and Rosemary Clooney. I found him to

ght
ermuda,
[19]67. Allan
[St]anley and
[Vic] Ash are
[se]cond and
[thi]rd from left;
[co]median
[Br]uce
[Fo]rsythe and
[hi]s wife
[Pe]nny Calvert
[ar]e at right;
[al]so two
[fe]male pas-
[se]ngers
[u]nknown).

[Ri]ght Phil Phillips Quartet
[at] the Talk of the Town,
*[19]69-70: Cyril Bevan
*[(d]rums), Phillips (piano),
*[P]A, John Ryan (electric
[ba]ss).

Left With
vibraphonist
and pianist
Victor
Feldman
in Los
Angeles,
the 1970s.

Above left With trumpeter Stan Roderick and Frank Sinatra, 1980. Frank was receiving a trophy to celebrate 10 years performing with his British orchestra.

Above right Pompeii, 199 with Helen Ash and Frank Sinatra Jr.

Left The Sinatra Orchestr at the Royal Albert Hall in 1980. Vinnie Falcone Jr conducting; Dougie Robinson, VA and Ronnie Ross (reeds); Tony Mottol (guitar). Sinatra is seated the centre, listening.

Below Egypt, 1979, Sinat (in white), Al Viola (guitar) Gene Cherico (bass), Vic bending in foreground.

Above left With Laurie Lewis (violin) and Shirley MacLaine on her 1977 European Tour. *Above right* With Tony Bennett at the Royal Albert Hall in 1999.

Above BBC Big Band in 1998 at the Queen Elizabeth Hall, London, with singer Stacey Kent and bandleaders/arrangers Ray Anthony, Billy May and Les Brown. (VA is first on left). *Below* BBC Big Band, 1994 at the Birmingham Symphony Hall with George Shearing at the piano and VA directly behind singer Mel Tormé.

Above With American clarinettist Eddie Daniels and Helen Ash at Eddie's New York apartment, April 1998.

Right Receiving an award from the Sinatra Music Society, London, 1986.

Below Left: With friend and fellow reeds player Iain Dixon at a BBC Big Band rehearsal in the early 1990s.

Below right A family band, with grandchildren Adam, Katie, Victoria and Jessica.

be an intensely private man, retreating with his valet into a special tent erected at the side of the stage during intervals. With hindsight I can see that when he did Parkinson's show he was not a well man; I played for the show at the BBC's Maida Vale studios which was his very last engagement, and he died two days later on a golf course in Spain. A plaque hangs in the studio to commemorate the television recording. When you mention Crosby you think of Bob Hope and he was also on the show, full of life with his gags coming as fast as ever.

Some of the artists that I met were approachable, others proved less forthcoming, but most of them were OK and, if they were really big names, I would get their autographs. Working closely with these greats had not warped my enthusiasm, and Parkinson's show gave me the opportunity to meet the very person I had idolised since first going to the cinema with my family in the late thirties. He was one of my all time heroes, and understandably my favourite *Parkinson* guest – Fred Astaire. Since I was a child with dreams of becoming a tap dancer I had been a fan of Astaire and when I was asked to do a rehearsal at Maida Vale Studios for his appearance on *Parkinson* I was in heaven. The only people in the studio were Harry Stoneham's group and the producer, and we eagerly awaited Fred's arrival.

When he walked in I was absolutely gobsmacked. Like Sinatra he brought an aura, a feeling of authority and greatness. In my career I have worked with literally dozens of big names so it might be easy to get a bit blasé about things, but with Fred Astaire and Sinatra my insides would always crumble – I was still a fan at heart.

Fred's daughter Ava had flown over from Ireland to be with him and she sat and listened as he sang a whole medley of songs from his movies, which Harry Stoneham had arranged for him. He had not danced in some years and although by no means a great singer he had a relaxed phrasing that swung along. It was one of the real highlights of my career to finally get to perform with my first hero. As he went through those wonderful songs I would look up from my music stand and just gaze at his feet.

Parkinson was great fun for me, as was another television series I did in the early eighties, also with Harry Stoneham: *The Bob Monkhouse Show*, which we used to record at the television studios in the old Shepherds Bush Empire. Bob was one of the nicest and funniest men you could hope to meet with wide ranging interests and an incredible memory. He too managed to lure some great guests on to the show, including Alice Faye, Sid Caesar and the perennially youthful Bob Hope.

13

Marriage, Fixing, and St. Paul's

With the advent of the eighties things began to change. And the biggest and best change of all was in my personal life. I went to a party one night in London, in the City, and across a crowded room (!) I saw a most attractive woman in a red dress. 'Out of your reach, Vic,' I told myself but to my surprise she came up to me and said she knew I was a musician, and we began talking. Although not particularly a jazz fan, Helen loved music and had been taken to shows from the time she was two. She was especially fascinated by songwriters and had an immense library of their biographies. Helen was divorced and had two children: Paul then at Leeds University, and Susannah who was an administrator in between doing lots of travelling. I too was divorced.

We went out a couple of times for a drink but I was afraid to push it too far, so we just saw each other occasionally for around a year until we met again at a party in New Malden in Surrey. We had then both ended previous relationships and we just talked and talked. This time I was not going to hold back and I phoned her the next day to make a date.

Before I knew it I was in love with her. We had booked a holiday together in southern Italy and I told Allan Ganley that I would take the opportunity to propose. What did he think? He had met Helen and liked her enormously so he said: 'Go for it.' So, by a fountain in a square in Rome I asked Helen if she would like to make our relationship permanent. A huge smile beamed across her face and we immediately began to plan our wedding. On the way home we called at her parents and, while Helen pretended to be busy in the bathroom, I formally asked her father if he had any objections to our marriage. A similar smile beamed across his face and immediately out came the whisky.

We were married on 5 September 1982 opposite Lord's Cricket Ground – very appropriate as Helen is a keen cricket fan. Life since then has been beyond my wildest imaginings. Paul and Susie both have children of their own. I think of them all as my own children and grandchildren, and I know they think of me the same way. Paul's son Adam is learning to play the clarinet and his beautiful daughter Katie is learning the drums. Susie's husband is French and they live in France. Her daughters, Jessica and Victoria, adore music too and Helen has introduced them to musicals. Jessica in particular asks to see them whenever she comes over; *Gypsy* is her favourite so far.

Coinciding with my personal happiness came the need to make a living in a different world. By the mid-1980s, at the same time as big touring artists were reducing their use of full orchestras, television shows found less space for live musicians and the session world was already starting its decline. In the rampant pop world, why use forty musicians when a couple of machines would provide the desired sound? So I had to think about yet another change of direction.

Although I had done a couple of brief runs in the past I had never liked the repetitiveness of London theatre work. Limited runs were more acceptable to me and I did enjoy doing *Beecham* at the Apollo Theatre with Timothy West in the lead role of Sir Thomas Beecham. I had to put on my classical boots for there was only me on clarinet, plus a cello, a violin and a piano. We had good fun with this. Timothy threw a nice party for the cast at the end of the run and his delicious wife Prunella Scales turned up too.

I also did *Privates on Parade* at the Piccadilly Theatre with Nigel Hawthorne and Denis Quilley in the cast and this was hilarious. The play was about a troupe of army entertainers, nearly all of whom were homosexual, who called each other by girls' names. Because the male characters were addressed that way the band adopted this too. I became 'Victoria' and Lennie Bush became 'Leonora'. Whenever any of the band for that show meet, to this day, we always call each other by our female names; jokingly of course!

Many of my musician colleagues were going into theatre work and so, when I was offered the chance to play for *42nd Street* at Drury Lane Theatre, I thought I would give it a go. I stayed in the orchestra for a couple of years but after the first few weeks I only did the two shows on Wednesdays and Saturdays and depped the other shows out. Several theatre musicians would gather together between shows at the tiny La Barocca restaurant in Moor Street, Soho, and drink enough wine to dull the pain of playing the same music every night. When the show ended I determined never to do theatre work again. I kept to this until the time I saw *City of Angels*, with Cy Coleman's exciting music turned into a pulsating jazz score by the great American arranger Billy Byers. I was so excited by this that I actually offered to do any deps just to play the music and I did a dozen or so performances of this show.

Another line of work began to open up as well. In 1982 I bumped into my dear friend Pete Moore, who is one of the finest arrangers in the country. Pete has arranged albums for Bing Crosby, Fred Astaire and Peggy Lee, to name just a few, and is very highly regarded in the business on both sides of the Atlantic. More importantly, he is one of the kindest, most self-effacing men you could wish to meet. Pete told me that the fixer he had been using had died and he wondered if I would like to fix his bands for any future recording sessions, as I knew 'everyone in the business'. This was unexpected but I considered it and said I would love to and got myself put on the Union books as a fixer as well as a player.

I have not done a great deal of fixing – a few small group recordings or concerts and the occasional big band – but I have always enjoyed this side of the business and it is a pleasure to work with Pete and with Ken Barnes, who frequently produces the albums.

There is an American singer called Jimmy Roselli, who is a most colourful man with a colourful life story. He was brought up in the same town as Sinatra and similarly knew many Mafia faces. Jimmy was doing very well as a young singer when one day he was asked to sing at a Mafia birthday party. Jimmy refused as he was booked to sing elsewhere that day. They kept insisting and he kept apologising until they put the phone down with the words, 'Be there.' Jimmy refused to be intimidated – he is very much his own man – and did not turn up for the party. The following day all Jimmy Roselli records had disappeared from every juke box in town. That was long ago and he now does very well, with dozens of best selling albums – his most famous song being

'When Your Old Wedding Ring Was New'. Back in the seventies he was commanding one hundred thousand dollars a night. He also showed me a watch given to him by the Mafia don John Gotti.

Jimmy had used Pete Moore as his arranger for years and he decided to do an album in England. I was asked to book the orchestra for this recording. For someone who is not that well-known in England he has a devoted fan base and one remarkable fan, who ran fruit and vegetable stalls, decided he would showcase Roselli at the London Palladium on a Sunday night. The Palladium is very expensive to hire and a full orchestra costs a lot too, so, as this man was unknown to me (and the fixer is responsible for paying any musician he books), I insisted on having the money for the concert before I committed the band. He sent me a cheque and it bounced. I phoned him and he said he had written it on the wrong account but, as time was getting short and there was no time to clear a new cheque, he would pay cash. As I was busy working, my wife had to go to Warren Street tube station and look for a nearby flower stall. When she reached there, the man in charge handed her an envelope with several thousands of pounds in it, all in very crumpled notes. The concert was a surprising success and the audience, largely from the East End, were dressed up to the nines – we were quite dazzled by all the sequins.

The American jazz record label Concord also approached me to fix an orchestra for a Scott Hamilton Christmas album and I have also booked orchestras for several new singers.

In 1982 I was also involved in a mammoth epic at St Paul's Cathedral. Channel 4 television, then a new and controversial network in UK broadcasting, staged an ambitious recreation of Duke Ellington's sacred music, the series of religious works which comprised some of his best writing from the last period of his life. Ellington's religious beliefs had always coloured his music but with the sacred music they assumed an almost obsessive prominence, especially so when he learned he was terminally ill during the early 1970s.

Ellington had stated that he wished his music to be performed in all the major religious structures around the globe and he had even taken his orchestra to the Taj Mahal in India in the late sixties. Channel 4's budget for the production was astronomical and we all received extremely good pay for our three days of extensive rehearsal and the final concert recording.

The orchestra was under the leadership of Bob Hartley, Yorkshire Television's principal musical director, and the personnel was a veritable who's who of post-war British jazz, bringing mainstream and more modern musicians together. Kenny Baker led the trumpet section, which also included Kenny Wheeler; Bobby Lamb was in the trombones, and in the saxes we had John Surman on baritone, Tony Coe on alto, Ronnie Scott on tenor and me on First Tenor and clarinet. Stan Tracey was on piano. There was a glittering array of guest stars: Tony Bennett, the Swingle Singers, Jacques Loussier, McHenry Boatwright (the bass-baritone opera singer who was married to Ellington's sister), Phyllis Hyman (who was the Broadway star of the Ellington show *Sophisticated Ladies*) and Douglas Fairbanks Jr; the evening was compered by actor Rod Steiger.

Despite this impressive line-up, my happiest memories of the occasion are the three days I spent with Ronnie Scott before the final televised concert. Friendly as we were, we had never shared the stage with such regularity and we would drive back to the club together after rehearsals finished, eat and drink and generally have fun. Ronnie loved watching television (the set was always on in his office) and also playing chess, but one of his greatest loves was gambling. He also loved movies and knew all the names of the old B-movie actors. His sense of humour was outrageous and he was one of the funniest men I ever met. When he leaned up against the pillar in the club telling the same old jokes his deadpan timing made us fall about laughing. He also liked to seize on unusual or foreign words and make a whole performance out of trying different pronunciations, accents and meanings.

Ellington's writing could veer from the simple to the complex and Ronnie, never as skilled at reading music as he was at improvising it, would get hopelessly lost. Bent over his music stand, his glasses slipping down his nose, he would frantically whisper to me from the side of his mouth, 'Vic, where the fuck are we?' We would soon both be virtually helpless with barely suppressed laughter.

We were both delighted to be sharing the stage with such names as Fairbanks and Steiger, and Steiger certainly did not disappoint us. Ronnie and I cornered him backstage and asked him if he would repeat his impersonation of W. C. Fields for us, as we had both loved his performance as the great actor-comedian in the 1976 movie *W. C. Fields and Me*. To our delight he *became* W. C. Fields, quoting lines from the movie absolutely brilliantly.

After Fairbanks had opened the show with a few words about Ellington and his religious inspiration, he made way for Steiger. Rod had obviously had plenty to drink on the night of the concert and he adopted a peculiar trembling mock-ecclesiastical tone and began referring to Duke Ellington as 'Duke Wellington'. We found it hard to control ourselves and I don't know what Duke's sister Ruth thought as she sat out front. I later learned that it had taken sixty-five hours of editing to cut out the superfluous 'W's.

The show had some spectacular dance sequences involving Wayne Sleep but the finale was a piece called 'David Danced' featuring tap dancer Will Gaines, who had actually worked with Ellington himself on some of the original sacred concerts. During his stay in London Will had been out on the town. He had got to know a whole group of youngsters and had asked them if they'd like to dance with him in his part of the show. Will had not thought it necessary to inform anyone else of this invitation, however. After he began the grand finale, it was planned that all the guest stars who were waiting patiently in line would take their bows. All this had been carefully choreographed.

Will began dancing, and he danced and he danced; and when we expected it all to end he motioned for his young friends to come and join him. Out came a very self-conscious bunch of kids who appeared to have little idea what was expected of them and they shuffled about the stage looking at the audience, who were as incredulous as we were. Gaines' feature was now beginning to seriously overrun and the television producers were signalling frantically. Bob Hartley brought the band into the close of the item but Gaines would just not stop. The guest stars were all looking at each other and wondering whether to leave the stage or begin their final walk on. He danced on alone as, one by one, his young friends crept awkwardly off the stage. Finally he threw off his hat and... stopped. The audience was stunned and silent and when the television recording came out it was still possible to see that something was wrong in spite of all the editing. What had been planned as a professional, respectful show had almost deteriorated into farce.

* * *

Ronnie Scott's death on 23rd December 1996 was a sudden and terrible loss. We were in Sydney on holiday at the time and my wife Helen was reading a newspaper when she suddenly gasped and cried, 'Vic! Oh my God, Ronnie Scott is dead.' Instantly it brought back all the experiences I had enjoyed with Ronnie, stretching from his encouragement in my early days to the last time we had met in the previous year: I had been rehearsing one afternoon at the club when Ronnie's faithful business partner and friend Pete King sought me out and asked me to see Ronnie. Ronnie was in the throes of deep depression as botched dental work had curtailed his ability to play. He was also at the end of a romance and had always been very intense about his romantic relationships. I found him in his dimly lit backstage office, his legs on the desk, staring passively at a flickering television. He barely looked up and was obviously not inclined to share in small talk with me. We sat there together, with me wondering what I could do to boost his morale. Then Ronnie looked at me and said, 'I can't play any more. I doubt if there is a chance I'll ever be able to play again.' I began to talk about our shared heyday of the fifties but Ronnie could only remark that those days were gone and we were both now old men. He added, somewhat prophetically, 'I don't want to be seventy.'

He died just a month before his seventieth birthday. There were nearly a thousand people at his memorial service at St Martin in the Fields in central London, including many musicians and celebrities who had come to give him a good send off. Benny Green and John Dankworth gave orations and there was lots of music and laughter. Ronnie would always call me Victory, and I dubbed him Ronaldo. He did a great deal for jazz in this country and he was one of our finest sax players, as well as being a very funny man who is much missed. He leaves an enduring legacy in the club, which has been brilliantly run by Pete King and is probably the best-known jazz club in the world. Pete has recently retired and Ronnie Scott's is being thoroughly refurbished. I just hope the new owners can keep the magic going.

Another face who is no longer with us is Benny Green. Benny, Harry Klein and I were very friendly back in the fifties and we used to go to Benny's flat in Cleveland Street, near what is now called Fitzrovia. Although he had played baritone in Ronnie's nine-piece band, he never really made it as a sax player. I co-led a band with him for a short while in the mid-fifties but he more or less stopped playing quite early to get into his career as author, journalist and broadcaster. He wrote books on music, cricket, theatre and London and his breadth of knowledge was awe-inspiring. His premature death in 1998 was another sad parting.

14

The BBC Big Band

During the eighties I frequently deputised in the BBC Big Band in London, both on its recordings for radio broadcasts and on its live shows. This arrangement suited me well. I would get a phone call at eight in the morning, always on time, and the manager of the orchestra would ask if I was working that day. If I was not, he would tell me who I would be deputising for and I would then make my way to Maida Vale Studios for the recording, or to Golders Green Hippodrome occasionally when the shows were recorded with a live audience. At the time I was living in Temple Fortune so I could easily walk to Golders Green.

I always enjoyed playing with the band. The music was always good, with excellent charts, and the musicians were first rate. I really liked playing in the middle of the saxophone section. So, when Pete Warner, who was the First Tenor, decided he wanted to leave the band and the baritone saxophonist Bernie George asked me how I would feel about joining on a full-time basis, I felt very enthusiastic. My initial thought was that the BBC would not take me on at my advanced age of fifty-eight because they normally retired their staff at sixty, but I reasoned that if they did accept me I would have two years of regular work. My second thought was to find out if the conductor Barry Forgie and the other sax players wanted me to join. They did. So I joined and I've been kept on as a freelance ever since.

The BBC had a tradition of maintaining an in-house band that stretched back to Henry Hall's orchestra in the thirties through to Cyril Stapleton's showband from the fifties. The BBC Big Band proper had started in 1970 and during its first decade had boasted some formidable jazz talents, including pianist John Horler, saxophonist Jimmy Hastings and trumpeter Alan Downey. When I joined in 1988 the saxophone section had Barry Robinson and Gordon Keats on alto, Nigel Nash on tenor and Bernie George on baritone.

The band held auditions for would-be members but they didn't ask me to do one because I had played with them so many times in the past and they knew what I could do. I've been on the panel of judges several times when players have been auditioning for the band and I really felt for those sax players who came in and played their best pieces for us and hoped it was good enough. When the Second Tenor chair became available with Nigel Nash's departure I was on the panel to audition prospective players and this was when I first came across Iain Dixon. He was very young at the time but already a fantastic saxophonist – we were all enthralled at his skill. He was a creative soloist as well as a good sight- reader, and he took his audition with the kind of delightful off-handedness that he would show even when he was confronted by the most tortuously complex music. It won him the job and admiration from the rest of us.

Iain and I quickly became friends and we developed what I would call a father and son relationship. He was always complimentary about my playing and I was over the moon about his. We must have cut very different figures seated together in the studios: me approaching sixty and rather conservatively dressed, Iain with his flowing hair and in such casual gear and that he would make a Hell's Angel look smart. Our meeting place was the music.

Working in a big band had not altered much from when I had been part of the John Dankworth's orchestra twenty years before. It still meant one-nighters in far-flung places but the whole thing was smoothed out by far-sighted planning and immaculate organisation. The band itself was the same kind of mix as the others I had played in: differing personalities who would come together to make the music happen. Young Mike Smith was one of the best big band drummers I had encountered. When Bernie George left for health reasons, former Buddy Rich sideman Jay Craig joined on baritone. Since then the sax section has changed and now includes, in addition to Jay and me, Howard McGill and Martin Williams, who are both great jazz soloists, and young Sammy Mayne.

Presiding over everything was Barry Forgie who is not only a fine conductor but a gifted arranger. The band also had the services of Sheila Tracy, ex-Ivy Benson trombonist and very knowledgeable writer on jazz and big bands, and she presented the ensemble on its regular radio series, *Big Band Special*, on Radio 2's Monday night jazz schedule. Sheila has a beautiful warm voice and struck a fine balance between being an expert, on the one hand, and an enthusiastic fan, on the other.

The Big Band has an incredible library of arrangements to pick from and we can use music from the swing charts of the thirties right up to contemporary works by writers like Bob

Mincer and Frank Mantooth. Joining the organisation gave me personally a great deal of exposure; people listen to the broadcasts and hear the soloists' names mentioned and then they will often come up to me when I am doing one of my own solo guest appearances and say, 'I listen to you with the BBC Big Band.'

The reputation of the band is such that guests are eager to be featured with it. We had home-grown talents such as Georgie Fame, Kenny Baker, Tina May and Peter King and legendary figures from the USA including big band era drummer Louis Bellson and great jazz soloists like Bob Brookmeyer, Benny Golson, Conte Candoli and Bobby Watson. More recently there have been guest vocalists such as Natalie Cole, Diana Krall, Patti Austin and the New York Voices.

For me, one of the greatest talents to appear with the band was our own Roy Castle. Roy guested with us on several occasions and, in addition to his singing and trumpet playing, tap danced on the radio! He was one of the nicest men one could hope to meet and had he been more ambitious and less of a family man he could have attained international stardom. I have recordings of him singing with Mel Tormé and with big American bands and he sounds truly amazing. I am still so sad that we lost him at such a young age.

In the summer of 1992 the BBC Big Band was booked to play a fund-raising concert in the grounds of Salisbury Cathedral (the Cathedral spire is the tallest in England and needed urgent restoration). Two guest stars were featured, the first being Rosemary Squires, an acclaimed vocalist who had found fame with a song called 'Frankfurter Sandwiches' back in the fifties. She was still much in demand and her warm and perfectly in-tune voice was behind the long running Fairy Liquid television commercial 'Hands that do dishes…'.

The second guest was Sir Edward Heath, the former British Prime Minister, who had made a sideline out of his love of classical music by becoming an occasional orchestral conductor. For this concert Heath was to conduct the Big Band on Artie Shaw's version of 'Begin the Beguine', which was a feature for me. During the afternoon run-through it became apparent to both of us that there was a wide chasm between our musical worlds. I stepped to the front of the stage and was confronted by a bemused looking Heath who enquired, 'What do I do here? Shall I count it in or some-thing?' I told him that a simple in-tempo count of one, two, three, four, would be sufficient.

'All right, gentlemen,' said Heath in a loud voice, 'Here we go…' He then simply gabbled the count with no tempo, no rhythm – just one-two-three-four. Luckily we had Mike Smith on drums and he brought in the tempo and we fol-lowed. It took several more tryouts before we could relax and be confident that Heath knew how to do it.

The evening concert was due to be broadcast live on BBC radio, a practice that demands split second timing between numbers to guarantee that the whole programme fits into its allotted airtime. Rosemary Squires came on and sang with her usual professional style and exited to Sheila Tracy's announcement: 'And now, our very special guest will conduct the BBC Big Band with Vic Ash on clarinet playing Artie Shaw's version of "Begin the Beguine"… Will you please wel-come Sir Edward Heath!'

The statesman walked on looking resplendent in his evening dress, did a half bow of acknowledgment to the applause and turned to face the band. I was already out front at the microphone and saw a look of distraction pass across Heath's face. He just stood there, half smiling and did nothing. The band was poised ready to play and they looked up wondering what was going to happen. It must have been a full thirty seconds (a lifetime on radio) that we waited in silence until in desperation I said, 'All right Ted? Shall we go?' The band fell about laughing, much to the bewilderment of the audience who had not heard what I said, and Heath seemed to shake himself and come out of his stupor exclaiming, 'Oh right, Yes!'

After such a bad start he surprised us all with a near perfect count off and he beamed throughout the number.

The BBC Big Band's reputation spread across the Atlantic and in the same year as the Heath incident we did a short tour of the United States and Canada. Our guest was the great British-born pianist, George Shearing. He had been in the States since the late forties and had founded his own quintet, invented his own block-chord style, written a jazz hit 'Lullaby of Birdland' and recorded strings of best-selling albums. We had already met in the 1950s and the Big Band had previously worked with him on an all-star bill with vocalist Mel Tormé in London, but this three-week tour meant I had a chance to get to know him better. Shearing, like Ronnie Scott, delighted in puns and confessed he would like to record an album of Stephen Sondheim songs and call it *Come Up and See Me Sondheim*. A great cricket fan, he set us all finding standard song titles that could become cricketing puns such as 'Gatting to Know You', 'On the Atherton, Topeka and Santa Fe' and 'Brearley Beloved'.

Although resident in New York, George and his wife Ellie rented a cottage each summer in Stow-on-the-Wold in the Cotswolds and one day my wife and I were invited there for tea. It was an idyllic day as we sat in the garden inhaling the scent of roses and soon George beckoned me inside, saying, 'I'm just about to do an album with Bob Farnon. What do you think of this?' and he proceeded to play 'Heather on the Hill' in his inimitable style on an old upright piano in that charming old-world cottage. I have rarely been so moved.

During the North American tour we all sat on the coach making up stupid word games to divert attention from the tedious journeys. We invented an imaginary orchestra staffed by performers like trumpeter Izzy Sharpe, vocalist Norma Stitz and manager Robin Bastard! The first week we zigzagged from north to south, from east to west, in such an illogical manner that I wondered if the New York promoters had ever seen an atlas. For those of you who have seen movies of musicians travelling on buses, I'll mention that we do *not* get out our instruments and play; we just nod off and complain and make up silly games or play poker.

Musically the tour was a total success and most of the venues were a sell-out. We were invited to receptions and went to out-of-the-way places like Kalamazoo in Michigan and New Bedford in Massachusetts, as well as to bigger cities like Chicago and Toronto. In Toronto I was able to catch up with my old bandleader Paul Heimann who came with his wife to see the concert. I had him announced from the stage and he stood up and took a bow and looked decidedly chuffed at this brief moment of fame. The tour was draining to all of us – in three weeks we only had three days off and on those it rained. The Americans were incredibly hospitable but all that any of us wanted to do was go back to the hotel and sleep.

* * *

After we returned to England in 1992 internal politics at the BBC seemed to signal the end of the Big Band. The plan had been to axe the band in the wake of so many BBC orchestras of the past but there was strong opposition from fans and we musicians gave a bus-top performance outside Broadcasting House and handed over a petition against the proposed cuts. The arguments carried on during 1994 until finally an agreement was reached whereby the name of the band was retained, as was the regular broadcast work, but the organisation would now be run by its own internal management instead of by the BBC. In effect, it would make all the musicians freelancers instead of employees. I was a freelancer anyway and was glad to know that the band would continue in some form or other.

Soon after, Iain Dixon left to concentrate on his jazz career. His was the classic dilemma of a big band musician seeking more musical freedom, the very same feelings which had fuelled the bebop revolution of the forties and which I could well sympathise with. I admired his willingness to give up the security of the BBC Big Band to further his own musical calling. I still think Iain is the best of the young players and I am joined in my opinion by the great American saxophonist Michael Brecker, who uses Iain on his recordings.

At the present time the Big Band boasts a great rhythm section with Jim Watson on piano, Tom Gordon on drums, Phil Robson on guitar and Anthony Kerr on vibes. We also have a great trombone jazz soloist in Andy Wood and a great lead trombone in Gordon Campbell. Latterly we have been fortunate to have the services of Jiggs Whigham as conductor, who alternates with Barry Forgie. Jiggs is an American trombone player who used to play with Stan Kenton and is now also a professor of music at a university in Germany. We are also lucky in having strong support for the band from BBC producer Bob McDowall, who oversees all our broad-casts and recorded concerts and, for Radio 3, from Keith Loxham.

Recently the band did a concert abroad and one of our trombone players missed the flight. We noticed the promot-er moving around counting heads and, to avoid any trouble, our librarian, Simon Lowy, borrowed Jiggs' trombone and sat in the section miming for the whole show. During rehearsal the soundman was looking most concerned at the lack of sound from that trombone chair but Simon assured him, 'I play softly.'

In the early nineties I was doing quite a few club appear-ances and concerts with my own group and many people would ask me when I was going to issue a CD, reminding me that it had been some thirty years since I had recorded a complete jazz album with my group. My wife and friends kept urging me to make a CD too so I began to consciously consider it.

The clincher came when I was working at the Barbican with Malcolm Creese, the bassist, and he told me he had started his own record label, was trying to build it up and would love me to do a quartet CD for it. Malcolm is a fine musician in both the classical and the jazz worlds; he is also a perfectionist so I knew I would be in good hands.

The next thing was to decide which tunes to record, because practically every worthwhile melody had been recorded to death. I had some tunes I knew I wanted to record but Helen had ideas for more unusual ones. She is always trying to persuade me to play beautiful but largely unknown melodies and for the CD I agreed to do 'Namely You' written by Gene de Paul from the show *Lil Abner*. I think Sonny Rollins recorded it but it was unknown to me. Most of the CD consisted of standards like 'I Thought About You', 'Soon', and 'Nancy with the Laughing Face' but Allan Ganley and I each came up with originals.

Allan was my natural choice as drummer; he had returned from Bermuda in the late seventies and taken up where he left off as one of Britain's best jazz musicians. He was able to provide skeletal arrangements which gave the CD some structure whilst allowing for the improvisations. Malcolm Creese wore two hats as producer and bassist and the elegant Dave Newton agreed to be my pianist. Dave has accompanied such notable players as Art Farmer and Benny Carter and has a wide-ranging style and a most delicate touch. He is one of England's finest jazz pianists and a particular favourite of mine.

I split the session fairly equally between tenor sax and clarinet and it was recorded at Porcupine Studios in South London in November 1994. We tried to do each tune in one take with no editing; we would do a take and if anyone wasn't happy with their contribution we would do another. In this way we managed to do the whole CD in two sessions in the one day.

Malcolm came up with the CD title *The Eyes Have It*, which combines a political pun with the fact that my eyes are two different colours. I used this title for one of my originals, an up tempo blues. My other original, 'November Rose' is a pensive, more broody number, which has recently been used behind an interview on the DVD of the film *Meet John Doe*. My recording of 'Nancy with the Laughing Face' has also been used on a DVD, Frank Sinatra's *Suddenly*.

The release coincided with my sixty-fifth birthday and forty-fifth year as a professional musician and I was quite

CD insert for *The Eyes Have It*, issued in 1995.

unprepared for the surge of interest when the album was issued. Every review was highly favourable, everyone saying it had been far too long since I had made an album of my own. The CD even penetrated the *Daily Telegraph*'s music pages when columnist, now famous author, Tony Parsons gave it a wonderful review. Many people phoned the paper asking where they could buy a copy. If I have to describe the album I would say it was the sort of 'dinner jazz' often heard on the radio – ideal background music for a candle-light meal – but it has been played on various radio jazz shows so perhaps there is more to it. It has sold well and is still selling.

The BBC commemorated my double anniversary by turning over an edition of *Big Band Special* in May 1995 entirely to

features by me. In an interview on *Jazz Notes* I told Digby
Fairweather that I intended to work as long as the phone
rang and as long as I felt I was able to maintain my own standards. I am often asked to do another CD, but there are so
many quartet albums around and if I did one I would want it
to be with strings. If dreams came true I would simply select
my favourite tunes and ask Johnny Mandel or Jeremy
Lubbock to arrange them for me. But that is a dream and, as
we no longer do the Lottery I can't see it coming true.

RADIO 2

BBC RADIO FM
88 · 90.2
MHz

8.30 Big Band Special
Sheila Tracy presents the
BBC Big Band, conducted
by Barry Forgie, in a
celebration of the career of
saxophone section member
Vic Ash. Vic, who celebrated
his 65th birthday last
month, also celebrates 45
years as a professional
musician this year. His
career has included spells
with the bands of Kenny
Baker and John Dankworth
as well as accompanying
such jazz greats as Ella
Fitzgerald and Frank Sinatra.

15

Billy May and Doris Day

The BBC Big Band landed perhaps its biggest catch in late 1998 when it played several concerts with three great survivors from the big band era: Billy May, Les Brown and Ray Anthony.

Les Brown was the senior partner at eighty-six and it was hard to recognise him as the photogenic bandleader of forty years before. He had been leading his own bands since the thirties but had really made it big when he hired Doris Day in the early forties and she recorded 'Sentimental Journey' for him. Brown had never felt the Swing Era's decline as painfully as some because he had concentrated his efforts on retaining a first class dance band rather than attempting to play bebop. He also had a long association with Bob Hope and accompanied the comedian on his many tours around the globe entertaining US servicemen.

The junior partner was Ray Anthony who, even at age seventy-six, remained the handsome figure he had been during the fifties, when he was a Cary Grant look-alike. Anthony had begun his career as a sideman in Glenn Miller's civilian orchestra but after active service in the Second World War he started his own band, which rose to become one of the most popular orchestras of the 1950s. As a trumpet player his style was sweet and low as opposed to high and dramatic and it served him well as a signature sound in an era when formerly successful working bands were falling around him. His *Dream Dancing* LP series for Capitol Records, his marriage to the glamorous actress Mamie Van Doren and his own good looks made his career not that dissimilar to that of Harry James. Anthony has remained active across the latter part of the twentieth century, recording often and still making concert appearances, his trumpet playing unaltered by age.

The greatest thrill for me, however, was the presence of Billy May. He had started out as a trumpet player with several of the big swing names, including Glenn Miller, but he quickly gained his reputation as an arranger, with an original, sometimes humorous, style. He had done arrangements for just about every vocal star of note. He had also patented one of the most colourful devices in big band writing, the slurping saxes sound. Heart problems had meant a radical loss of weight and I had trouble in recognising him from the robust portly figure he used to be.

I made a beeline for him and told him how much I admired his work. We talked about Sinatra and in the middle of discussing the recordings May and Sinatra had made together, Billy stopped suddenly and asked, 'Say, you're not Vic Ash, are you?' He explained that he had given a talk to the Sinatra Music Society and that Marjorie Nunn, the organiser of the London branch, had mentioned that I had played with Sinatra and would be in the BBC band.

Billy was a very approachable guy, one of the chaps, not at all big-time, and he loved to answer questions about the music he had done with his own band and his wonderful albums, such as *Sorta May* and *Sorta Dixie*. His music is fun to play and written in such a way that it is not too difficult. But it's hard to do the slurping sax thing because, unless all the saxes do it at exactly the same time, it really can go awry. We've done it so many times in the Big Band that we have synchronised our slurps!

He was more or less retired when we talked in 1998 but he told me that Frank Sinatra Jr wanted him to do some arrangements. I am not sure whether he did them or not, and now this delightful man is no longer with us.

The concerts were a fantastic success with lines of people around the Royal Festival Hall hoping for returns.

Helen and I attend the monthly meetings of the Sinatra Music Society when we can. We usually get to their Christmas parties, with Frank singing 'We wish you the Merriest, the Merriest' as we walk in and Father Christmas coming down the chimney handing out presents to all of us – small gifts with Sinatra's name or face on them. They have a quiz about who sang what, which year such-and-such a record came out and there is a really great atmosphere. Former record producer Ken Barnes has now been banned from taking part in the quiz as his phenomenal memory means that he knows all the answers. I have given talks to the Society several times, usually after finishing a tour with Frank, and Helen gave a talk to them once on being an 'orchestra wife' and the highs and lows of that.

The 'high' for her was one time when she came to listen to the orchestra rehearse at the London Arena. By this time Sinatra never normally came to the rehearsals and Helen was sitting all alone in a vast auditorium listening to the music when she suddenly looked up and Sinatra was on stage. This was the first time he had played this venue and he stayed up there for over an hour singing song after song, many of which he had not sung for years and didn't use in the show. He was very funny, quipping with Frank Jr, and Helen sat there entranced, darting glances at me, half expecting to be thrown out but revelling in a concert for her alone. Another 'high' was sitting in the wings at the Paris Opera during *The Ultimate Event* tour, amongst all the sets for the operas, watching Liza Minnelli, Frank and Sammy Davis clown about on stage. Under the great chandelier, enjoying the show, were luminaries like Jacques Chirac and Gregory Peck. One of the boxes was so full of people that Helen kept expecting a body to tumble down.

Another story which the Society liked happened in Milan. Helen went into a shop and asked to look at dresses. The assistants asked what sort of dress she wanted and she said it was for the Sinatra concert that evening. 'How did you get tickets?' they asked and when she explained that her husband was one of the musicians, the shop went wild. All the staff came up from the basement and just goggled at Helen because she was the wife of one of Frank Sinatra's musicians. She says she could not have felt more important if she had been Mrs Frank Sinatra herself.

A large contingent from the Society always travelled to Sinatra's European dates and the members were there in force when we played Rotterdam. At the end of the show one of the other musicians nudged me and said, 'Look, Vic.' I turned round and there, marching towards the stage, was a group of people from the Society holding a large banner which had on it: 'Vic Ash Fan Club Rotterdam branch'. The American players thought I really was a big shot in Europe after this and were most impressed. Marjorie Nunn, a guiding light of the Sinatra Music Society, sadly died not long after Frank himself and is very much missed.

An artist with whom I've become very friendly over the years is the wonderful singer Rosemary Squires who sounds as clear, as swingy, as perfect today as she did fifty years ago. One day she and her husband Frank invited us to lunch and Helen suggested that Rosemary should do a show using the songs of Doris Day. Rosemary said the late Roy Castle had made the same suggestion to her but she was not sure where to start. Helen had been a huge fan of Doris Day while she was at school and had several books about her. She volunteered to start the ball rolling and draft out a preliminary script. Rosemary then worked on this and enticed ex-Ted Heath singer Dennis Lotis to join the package.

I formed a quartet with Clive Dunstall on piano, John Rhys Jones on bass and Chris Dagley on drums and we began to knock it into shape. Later Brian Dee replaced Clive on piano, Pete Cater took over on the drums and there were various bass players. We started off in Grays in Essex in October 1996 and toured all over the country with the show for seven years. The audience seemed to love it and sang along to the mainly standard tunes that Doris had sung. We had good arrangements by Don Innes and Dave Mostin, Rosemary's ex-manager, and I did a couple of jazz numbers in each half. We still get the occasional enquiry for the show so it could re-surface at some time, even though we are all doing different things now. Rosemary received a well deserved MBE in 2004 for her services to music and to charity.

16

Getting the Buzz

Since I started out in 1950 the music scene has changed a lot. Back then I was regarded as a modern jazz musician. There were the different schools of jazz: trad, dixie, swing and modern – but today I'm often described as a mainstream/modern player. Now of course there is contemporary jazz as well. Things have moved on and each little group of jazz styles has its following.

One of the other things I was extensively involved in over the years, the session world, has changed a lot too. The introduction of the first synthesisers about thirty years ago signalled its demise. Here was an instrument that could reproduce the sounds of many other instruments and it is not surprising that producers opted for an economically favourable option. Orchestras in the studios and television got smaller and the session world today, apart from film music, is mainly to do with pop music

Certainly one of the best things I've noticed in the last few years is the increasingly young audience for jazz. If I'm doing a guest appearance I often see young faces in the crowd. They may have heard of me, they may not, but it's nice to see them taking an interest in jazz. Many of these young people seem to be fascinated by the modern jazz era of the fifties and sixties. Even young musicians that I've worked with ask me to talk about the times I spent with Ronnie Scott, Tubby and Phil Seamen, to name a few, and some of them wish they had been around at the time. I consider myself lucky to have been born when I was; I grew up into a fantastic era of jazz with many wonderful musicians both in the States and here. It's strange in some ways to think how some of the old records command premium prices from the collectors. Even though they are now easily available on CD, the original vinyl Jazz Couriers albums by Ronnie Scott and Tubby Hayes are really coveted and I've been told that the Jazz Five album I did also fetches a premium price. Nobody at the time we did all those things, in the fifties and sixties, had any idea that forty years later they would be valuable collectors' items. We were just playing the music of the day.

The approach to learning to play jazz has changed too. I just used my ears and learned tunes but I do regret not having had any formal training. My friend Allan Ganley was helped a tremendous amount by his scholarship to Berklee back in the sixties. I would have liked the opportunity to learn more theory, more about chords, harmony and arranging. When I began, a few of the guys studied theory with Denis Rose, who had great theoretical knowledge, but most of us just earned and learned. There were no big bands you could join and blow with; you just sat in with other musicians wherever you could and copied things off records. I think we all set out to copy one chosen player. Ronnie Scott got heavily into Stan Getz, whereas I was really into Buddy De Franco. Without even realising, you tend to copy someone –

all you can do is try to put your own thing into it. Everybody has something that marks them out and you have to try and find it. Here in Britain there is still a degree of comparison between our players and the Americans – just as in the fifties when we had people who were referred to as 'England's answer to...', or 'Britain's version of...'; Getz and Zoot clones, if you like. We still have imitators, but jazz in this country is in safe hands for the future. We have some wonderful players. That is not just referring to the younger guys like Gerard Presencer, Mark Nightingale and Iain Dixon, but to older players like Stan Tracey and Peter King who are world class.

I suppose that about 90 per cent of the younger players I work with have come through the National Youth Jazz Orchestra: Nigel Hitchcock, Dave O'Higgins, Jamie Talbot, Mark Nightingale, Martin Williams, Howard McGill – a whole bunch of them. NYJO, along with many other youth jazz orchestras, gives young musicians a solid grounding. They buy all the right charts (a lot of which we use with the BBC Big Band) and give great schooling to younger players. The high standard of a lot of these young musicians is something that many musicians of my age have never reached even after years of learning on the job. There will always be guys who don't want to play in the big bands: if you want to be a dixieland player, your main thing would be in a small band; but if you want to do a bit of everything, the big band provides wonderful experience.

To a degree I find that the players today are a little less personal than in my era. On tenor sax, for example, years ago if you had any kind of ear, you could pin-point who it was on the tenor: Stan Getz, Al Cohn, Ronnie Scott, Zoot Sims, Tubby Hayes, Johnny Griffin – they all had their own sound.

Even the ones who were in the same 'soft school' – Getz, Al and Zoot – were still recognisable. Today I find it difficult to pick out the individual players. I can recognise Mike Brecker but there are many others, all great contemporary players, that I can't pick out, because they all have that same sound and style, great as they are. I have great admiration for what they play, particularly Brecker. His technique, the way he plays through the changes, and his jazz improvisation are fantastic. I confess I find it difficult to identify the other tenors of today, apart from Joe Henderson, who was really between the two schools, hard and soft, and was a very lyrical player who I could recognise. When it comes to the hard school of tenor playing – the Bob Bergs, the Wayne Shorters, I would not be able to name them with confidence. There are a few players out on the US West Coast who are still doing great modern jazz but not quite going into the contemporary thing, like Tom Scott and Pete Christlieb. That's the kind of jazz I like listening to.

Speaking technically I have noticed that we are now finding it easier to play the modern arrangements; all the sax ensembles can be tricky but the phrasing is the way we phrase now. So when the band plays music of the thirties and forties, as we sometimes do, we find it more difficult because the phrasing was so different and the interpretation of it was also different. If you listen to some of the Paul Whiteman stuff of the twenties, some of the sax ensembles they used to play were unbelievable: fast tonguing to an incredible extent. It is easy to say now that the music sounds corny but at the time it was contemporary and they really needed to know how to read; it was heads down all the way. Maybe some of today's jazz will sound corny in forty years time. I can't see where it can go from here, because technically it has reached impossible limits, but who knows? In modern jazz and main-stream jazz we still rely on tunes. That's still my first love: the great standard melodies of Gershwin, Porter, Berlin, Kern, Warren, Arlen – will anyone of today rank alongside these geniuses?

I've noticed in the last few years or so that salsa music from Cuba is becoming immensely popular. It is on television commercials, salsa clubs are opening and it is very jazz orientated, particularly trumpet jazz with people like Arturo Sandoval. It's wonderful foot tapping, body moving music and it is great to see quality music being popular, but as far as standards go, I think there will always be guys playing them.

I have been playing jazz now for over fifty-five years but I haven't lost my admiration for my early heroes and I suppose Stan Getz still remains my overall idol out of all jazz players of any instrument. Probably his *Jazz at the Shrine* is the album for me, mainly because of the way that Getz and trombonist Bob Brookmeyer jell together. When that album was issued back in the fifties, I think that all jazz players – regardless of whether they played dixieland, swing, modern or whatever – loved that album. In my early days there were so few albums coming out that we all heard the same ones. I have collected records of my favourite singers and players since I was very young and marvelled at Woody Herman's band playing 'Caldonia', and at Buddy de Franco's 'Penthouse Serenade' and 'Lady be Good'. I used to think, 'My God, how do they do that?' in a way similar to how I now think about Mike Brecker and the incredible American clarinettist Eddie Daniels.

I imagine that the younger listeners like contemporary jazz and the older ones don't, but I could well be wrong.

When the BBC Big Band play university dates with contemporary conductors like Julian Joseph, we get a very young crowd who seem to understand the music better than the rest of us.

I am often asked if I am going to retire but Helen and I think that we should aim for a situation where I can pick and choose when I want to play. To some extent I do this now and I do enjoy the variety of work that I do. Helen says that working keeps my mind alive as I'm not a man for hobbies, so I had better stick at it. I love living in a pretty village in Buckinghamshire. I have a nice home, a wonderful wife, grandchildren, the full set. Sometimes when I have to go out at night to play, I ask myself why am I leaving my warm home to get in the car and drive all those miles to play? Ego! After fifty or so years I am still flattered at being asked and I hope the phone will keep ringing.

Music has always been my life to the exclusion of other things but lately I have begun to read more and would try and do more of that if work slowed down. Helen and I have always liked to travel and lately have taken to spending part of each year in Brisbane. We have many friends there, especially the wonderful Fallon family who have welcomed us as one of their own. We have also met up with Skip and Di Humphries. Skip was Head of Music for LWT in the eighties and Di was also heavily involved in the music scene. By a coincidence they live in the next building to where we rent an apartment. They are both funny and warm-hearted and we love to spend time going over the old days – as well as me telling them what is happening at the present time. We love the way of life and, of course, the sun. We hope to continue to do this but will stay based in England.

Music has provided me with security in life, which is not available to the young musicians of today. There are so many coming up – where will they all work?

I can't say I feel the 'buzz' as much as when I first came into the business. In the early fifties nearly every date was a buzz because I was doing so many diverse things all the time and it was all new and fresh. I do get the buzz occasionally even now. It was always a real thrill to do the Sinatra tours; they were twenty-two years of magic always. If I had to put it in percentage terms I should say that in those days it was a 95 per cent buzz, whereas today it's more like 50 per cent. I enjoy about half of what I do and the rest I'm thankful at having been asked to do it. When I've done a jazz date and it has been really good I feel like a different person, especially when I'm with such brilliant piano players as John Pearce, Geoff Eales. John Horler, John Critchinson or Brian Dee, to name just a handful. I come home and tell Helen that I feel elated. That is when I feel the buzz like I used to.

I feel I have developed musically through the years and on the rare occasions when I listen to an old recording of mine, I can tell that my technical proficiency has improved and that my improvising has broadened. This is possibly because I play so much with younger players and I'd like to think that I have matured as a player rather than changed completely, and that I'm still recognisable as me.

I am often asked to pick out a single special moment in my career. I'm very proud to have worked with so many great artists over the years and have done so many different things that it becomes hard to single out one special moment. I suppose that the concert I did at the Royal Festival Hall with my quartet in 1956 comes close to being one of the most memorable. I can see it now – the packed

Just as this book goes to press: Vic with Allan Ganley's Big Band taking part in the summer festival at the Stables, Wavendon, on the afternoon of 25th June 2006. Allan Ganley (conducting), John Horler (piano) and Sam Burgess (bass). Vic is seated between fellow saxophone players Julian Siegel and John Dankworth.

house, the cheering, the standing ovation. That was really something for a twenty-six-year-old. Working with Sinatra was perhaps the high point, with the memory of standing up to play the solo on 'Pennies from Heaven' at the Royal Albert Hall, with Frank jigging around in time to me and then announcing my name – Vic *Sax*!

I've been lucky in having had such a long career and to be still playing with the BBC Big Band. When I think of those people I knew well who are no longer here, like Ronnie and Tubby and Victor Feldman, I know I've been very lucky. People come up to me and say, 'Vic Ash! I first saw you nearly fifty years ago and you're still playing!' I tell them, 'Yes, and I'm going to keep on doing it until I get it right.'

Chronology

1930   Born 9 March in Whitechapel, London.
1939   Evacuated to Sutton, Cambridgeshire.
1940   Returns to London in time for the Blitz. Evacuated again to Northamptonshire.
1944   Back in London. Joins Oxford and St George's Youth Club. Takes up the clarinet.
1945–6 Clarinet tuition with Charles Chapman while working as a salesman in the East End.
1948   Tour of British military bases in Germany in a band with Stan Tracey.
1950   Turns professional with Kenny Baker Sextet. Also in the band are Jimmy Skidmore and 15-year-old Tubby Hayes.
1951–2 First recording with Baker for Parlophone. Nominated in 1952 *Melody Maker* Critics Choice poll. Guests with Ted Heath Orchestra.
1953   Joins Vic Lewis Orchestra on clarinet and alto saxophone. Wins first *Melody Maker* Jazz Poll in clarinet category. Concert appearances in Iceland with own quintet.
1954   Leaves Vic Lewis to lead own quartet. Tours and records with singer Maxine Sullivan. First recording session as leader, for Melodisc.
1955–6 Wins *New Musical Express* poll as top clarinet player. Freelance jazz gigs as well as own group concerts. First TV series, *Teleclub*, with Steve Race. Tours with Hoagy Carmichael and Cab Calloway. Goes to USA on *Queen Mary*. Records with own group for Denis Preston. Triumphant concert at Royal Festival Hall.
1957   Briefly rejoins Vic Lewis in spring. Forms own quintet – Vic Ash and his Music. Takes quartet to USA in Musicians Union/American Federation Exchange deal. Begins to feature tenor saxophone.
1958   Forms sextet with Johnny Scott, Ian Hamer, Alan Branscombe. Takes band featuring Bert Courtley to USA on MU/AF exchange.

1959   Rejoins Vic Lewis on clarinet and tenor sax. Opens the bill on Jazz from Newport package with own quintet opposite Dizzy Gillespie, Buck Clayton, Dave Brubeck and Jimmy Rushing. Regular appearances on *Sunday Break* TV show.

1960   To USA with Vic Lewis All Star Orchestra including Dudley Moore. Plays at Birdland in New York City. Forms Jazz Five with Harry Klein. Tours opposite Miles Davis and with Carmen McRae. Records Jazz Five album *The Five of Us*, released in the States on the Riverside label. Plays at the new Ronnie Scott Club.

1961   With Jazz Five. Tours opposite Dave Brubeck Quartet.

1962   Takes up flute. Disbands Jazz Five. Joins Dankworth Orchestra on tenor sax and clarinet. Records single 'Banco'. Last (8th) win on *Melody Maker* clarinet poll.

1963   Joins Bill Russo's London Jazz Orchestra. Two weeks in England and France with the Ray Charles Orchestra. Records *What the Dickens* and makes first film soundtrack with Dankworth Orchestra.

1964   Records with Dankworth Orchestra on *Zodiac Suite*.

1965   Records BBC TV *Jazz 625* with Dankworth Orchestra and guests Clark Terry and Bob Brookmeyer. Gigs with Grischa Farfel.

1966–9 Moves to Bermuda in 1966 to join Joe Wylie's band. Returns to London in March 1969.

1970   First tour with Frank Sinatra. Joins Phil Phillips for seven years at Talk of the Town.

1971–9 Tours with Sinatra and plays with Bing Crosby, Peggy Lee, Jack Jones, Tony Bennett, Liza Minnelli, Shirley MacLaine, Carpenters, etc. Michael Parkinson's TV show with Harry Stoneham. Studio and session work.

1979   Sinatra concert in Egypt, at the Pyramids.

1980–7 More Sinatra tours. Freelance jazz gigs. In Ronnie Scott's orchestra accompanying Ella Fitzgerald. Studio, concert, TV, film and club work.

1988   Joins BBC Big Band as First Tenor.

1992   Last Sinatra gig with John Dankworth and Cleo Laine. Tour of USA with BBC Big Band and George Shearing.

1993   Reunited with Kenny Baker for special engagement and recording at Ronnie Scott's Club in Birmingham.

1994   Records his first CD *The Eyes Have It* with Allan Ganley, Dave Newton and Malcolm Creese.

1995–today Still with BBC Big Band. Gigs with Tony Bennett, Ray Charles, Billy May, Ray Anthony and Les Brown, Robert Palmer, Jamie Cullum; appearance on BBC TV *East Enders*. Remains in demand as a jazz soloist, big band player, session man, contractor and with his own quartet.

Discography

This brief discography details all of Vic's jazz recordings as a leader or co-leader. In compiling it I drew heavily on W. Bruyninckx' *Swing Discography* (1985) and on Vic's own copies of the relevant recordings and memories of the sessions.

Happily, several of Vic's vintage recordings have recently been reissued on CD by the Jasmine label: his debut recordings as a leader in his own right, originally released on the Melodisc label can be found on *Bop-in Britain Volume 2 – Gettin' The Message* (JASCD 638); the National Jazz Federation's 1956 Festival Hall concert recorded for the Tempo label has reappeared on Jasmine JASCD 614 *Modern Jazz Scene 1956* and a further Tempo session, perhaps Vic's finest record, the Jazz Five album *The Five of Us*, is now available on Jasmine JASCD 623.

Some examples of his work for producer Denis Preston, issued originally on the Nixa label, can be found on the 3-CD box set *Too Hot – The Best of Mainstream British Jazz* (Castle CMETD 992), including a title from the EP *Vic Ash + Four* featuring trombonist Keith Christie and drummer Phil Seamen, and a rare track from a *Melody Maker* Poll Winners album.

Enthusiasm for Vic's earlier work is shared by fans who still ask him about the sessions and in 1997 Tony Hall, Vic's one time producer at Tempo Records, wrote that the Jazz Five LP was 'the best sounding album I ever produced,' (*A Century of Jazz*, Hamlyn Books, 1997).

To compile a complete discography of Vic's recordings since his career began in 1950 would be an enormous task, and one that lies outside the scope of this autobiography. Indeed, whilst he has collected a great deal of what he has recorded in such circumstances, he can be forgiven for not having acquired everything, particularly during the glory days of his session period after his return from Bermuda in 1969 up until the 1980s. He describes his attendance in the recording studios at this time as having the regularity of 'guys going to the office' and there have been literally thousands of hours of recordings for films, television, albums and radio – far too much to capture in this brief summary.

During the course of research for this book I was fortunate to be privy to Vic's vast collection of tapes of radio broadcasts. Among them are real gems, including recordings with Tubby Hayes and a tape of the Stan Tracey Quartet with Vic in place of Peter King. On this he proves himself to be as sensitive an interpreter of the pianist's music as any of Tracey's regular saxophonists. Both the quality and quantity of such sessions illustrate how much room there was in the 1950s and 60s for jazz on the radio, a fact that Vic points out is sadly not the case today.

There are many privately recorded acetates from the late forties to mid-fifties that have Vic performing alongside musicians such as Eddie Thompson, Jimmy Deuchar and Stan Tracey. The handwritten labels tantalisingly give away scant details like '"Donna Lee" – Vic Ash + Don Rendell (1951)'. He gives assurance that one day he'll find the time to listen to them.

Simon Spillett
October 2005

LPs, EPs and CD Titles

Original releases of key records under Vic Ash's name

Vic Ash Quartet, *Session by Four*   Nixa/Polygon JTE 100 (EP)

Vic Ash, *Clarinet Virtuoso*   Columbia SEG 7634 (EP)

Vic Ash Quartet, *Hoagy*   Nixa NJE 1002 (EP)

Vic Ash Quartet, *Royal Festival Hall Modern Concert*

                                     Tempo EXA 44 (EP)

Tubby Hayes and his Orchestra, New Jazz Group, Vic Ash Quartet,

  British Modern Jazz Scene 1956   Tempo TAP 2 (LP)

Various artists, *Swingin' the Blues* Tempo TAP 21 (LP)

Vic Ash, *Love Letters*   MGM E 347 (LP)

Vic Ash Quintet, *Vic Ash Plus Four*

                                     Nixa NJE 1032 (EP)

Various artists, *All the Winners – Melody Maker Jazz Poll 1957*

                                     Nixa NJT 509 (LP)

Various artists, *Black Stick*   Nixa NJL 20 (LP)

Various artists, *All the Winners – Melody Maker Jazz Poll 1958/9*

                                     Nixa NJT 518 (LP)

The Jazz Five, *The Five of Us*   Tempo TAP 32 (LP)

  issued in the USA as *The Hooter* Riverside (Jazzland) RLP 361 (LP)

Vic Ash Quartet, *The Eyes Have It* Audio-B ABCD 3R (CD)

Recording Sessions

Vic Ash (clarinet), Gerry McLoughlin (vibes), Derek Smith (piano), Johnny Hawkesworth (bass), Allan Ganley (drums). London, February 16 1954.

DA 2009	*Softly as in a Morning Sunrise*	Melodisc 1286
DA 2100	*Ain't Misbehavin'*	Melodisc 1315
DA 2101	*Blue Room*	Melodisc 1286
DA 2102	*Lullaby of the Leaves*	Melodisc 1315

(All the above reissued on Jasmine JASCD 638)

Vic Ash (clarinet), Eddie Thompson (piano), Bill Sutcliffe (bass), Allan Ganley (drums). London, January 3 1955.

CM 353	*Good Bait*	Columbia DC 689, Columbia SEG 7634
CM 354	*Dream a Little Dream*	–
	Jeepers Creepers	Nixa JTE 100, Jazz Today JTS 1501
	Blue Jeans	–

Vic Ash (clarinet), Eddie Thompson (piano), Barry Hamilton (bass), Benny Goodman (drums). London, February 3 1955.

| *Cocktails for Two* | Nixa JTE 100, Jazz Today JTS 1501 |
| *I Hear Music* | – |

Vic Ash (clarinet), Bill Le Sage (piano), Sammy Stokes (bass), Phil Seamen (drums). London, July 26 1955.

Skylark	Nixa NJE 1002
Lazybones	–
The Nearness of You	–
Two Sleepy People	–

Vic Ash (clarinet), Eddie Thompson (piano), Bill Sutcliffe (bass), Benny Goodman (drums). London, October 20 1955.

| CM 405 | *I Got It Bad (And That Ain't Good)* | Columbia DC 710 |
| CM 406 | *Love Me or Leave Me* | Columbia SEG 7634,   – |

Vic Ash (clarinet), Laddie Busby (trombone), Max Harris (piano), Sammy Stokes (bass), Phil Seamen (drums), with small string section arranged and conducted by Laurie Johnson. London, 1955.

Love Walked In	MGM E 347
Love is Here to Stay	–
When your Lover has Gone	–
Almost Like Being in Love	–
When I Fall in Love	–
I'm in the Mood for Love	–
Like Someone in Love	–
Don't Say Love has Ended	–
Love Begins	–
Lover Man	–
Love for Sale	–

Vic Ash (clarinet), Terry Shannon (piano), Pete Elderfield (bass), Benny Goodman (drums). Royal Festival Hall, London, February 18 1956.

VOG 595 *Early Morning*		Tempo EXA 44	Tempo TAP 2
VOG 596 *Doxy*	Tempo TAP 21	–	–
VOG 597 *Blue Lou*		–	–
VOG 598 *Just One of Those Things*		–	–

(All the above reissued on Jasmine JASCD 614)

Vic Ash (clarinet), Keith Christie (trombone/valve trombone), Derek Smith (piano), Sammy Stokes (bass), Phil Seamen (drums). London, December 11 1956.

Cinders	Nixa NJE 1032	
You Took Advantage of Me	–	
Ash Felt	–	
With the Wind and the Rain in your Hair	–	Castle CME TD 992

Vic Ash (clarinet), Denny Termer (piano), Laurie Deniz (guitar), Sammy Stokes (bass), Cyril Sherman (drums). London, October 1957.

Softly as in a Morning Sunrise	Nixa NJT 509, Castle CME TD 992

Vic Ash (clarinet), Maurice Bielle (vibes), Stan Jones (piano), Arthur Watts (bass), Allan Ganley (drums). London, March 26 1958.

Blue 'n' Boogie	Nixa NJL 20
High Priest	–

Vic Ash (clarinet), Ian Hamer (trumpet), Johnny Scott (flute), Alan Branscombe (piano), Spike Heatley (bass), Dave Pearson (drums). London, September 1958.

One for the Boys	Nixa NJT 518

Vic Ash (tenor sax, clarinet), Harry Klein (baritone sax), Brian Dee (piano), Malcolm Cecil (bass), Bill Eyden (drums). London, October 23 1960.

Autumn Leaves	Tempo TAP 32	Riverside RLP 361
'Pon my Soul	–	–
There It Is	–	–
The Five of Us	–	–
(All the above reissued on Jasmine JASCD 623)		
Midsummer	rejected	

As above, but Tony Mann (drums) replaces Eyden. London, November 12 1960.

Hootin' *	Tempo TAP 32	Riverside RLP 361
Still Life	–	–
(Both reissued on Jasmine JASCD 623)		
*Retitled *The Hooter* on Riverside RLP 361		
Midsummer	rejected	

Vic Ash (clarinet, bass clarinet, tenor sax), Malcolm Cecil (bass), Johnny Scott (arranger, conductor), plus unidentified: three trombones, three french horns, piano, xylophone, drums and percussion. London December 17 1962.

Banco	Columbia DB 4997
Man of Action	–

Vic Ash (clarinet, tenor sax), Dave Newton (piano), Malcolm Creese (bass), Allan Ganley (drums). Mottingham, London, November 1994.

The Touch of Your Lips	Audio-B	ABCD 3
Bernie's Tune	–	
I Thought about You	–	
November Rose	–	
Between the Devil and the Deep Blue Sea	–	
Silver Minor	–	
Namely You	–	
Soon	–	
Carnival Samba	–	
Nancy with the Laughing Face	–	
The Eyes Have It	–	

Film Soundtracks

(with the score's composer and conductor):

The Servant	(John Dankworth)	1963
Darling	(John Dankworth)	1965
Modesty Blaise	(John Dankworth)	1966
Morgan, A Suitable Case for Treatment	(John Dankworth)	1966
Steptoe and Son	(Roy Budd)	1972
(also on-screen appearance)		
Wild Geese	(Roy Budd)	1978
For Your Eyes Only	(Bill Conti)	1981
84 Charing Cross Road	(George Fenton)	1986
All Dogs Go to Heaven	(Ralph Burns)	1989
Steppin' Out	(Peter Matz)	1991

Index

Abbey Road Studios, London, 106
Aberdeen, 15
Adderley, Cannonball, 15, 34
Alberghetti, Anna Maria, 86
Ali, Muhammad, 67
American Armed Forces Radio, 28
American Federation of Musicians, 20, 49, 54, 80
American Forces Network, 54
Anthony, Ray, 143-4
Apollo Theatre, Harlem, 53, 123
Archer Street, London, 18-19
Arlen, Harold, 98, 152
Armstrong, Louis, 40
Arthey, Johnny, 24
Ash, Helen, 56, 86-7, 89, 101-2, 110-1, 113, 121-2, 129, 139, 145-7, 153-4
Ash, Isaac and Sarah, 2-7, 9, 11, 16, 23, 28, 36-7, 85, 110
Astaire, Fred, 9-10, 91, 119-20, 124
Austin, Patti, 134
Baker, Chet, 40, 52, 59, 71
Baker, Kenny, 23-7, 36-7, 46, 75, 91, 93, 126, 134
Ball, Kenny, 11, 65
Barnes, Ken, 124, 145
Basie, Count, 13, 49, 52, 93, 106
BBC, 59, 79
    Big Band, 76, 82, 109, 131-45, 150-2, 155
    Television Centre, 115

Maida Vale Studios, 119
Beatles, 58, 79, 107
Beaulieu Jazz Festival, 65
Beck, Gordon, 72
Beecham, Sir Thomas, 123
Bellson, Louis, 134
Bennett, Tony, 80, 95, 109-10, 126
Benson, Ivy, 133
Berg, Bob, 151
Berklee College of Music, Boston, USA, 85-6, 149
Berlin, Irving, 9, 30, 152
Bermuda, 83-9, 106, 140
Bernstein, Leonard, 107
Berry, Chuck, 79
Bilk, Acker, 27, 37, 65-6
Birdland, New York, 52, 60-1
Boatwright, McHenry, 126
Boston, USA, 50.
Brand, Pat, 26
Branscombe, Alan, 52, 56, 74
Bray, Pete, 24, 26
Brecker, Michael, 51, 59, 80, 138, 151-2
Breen, Bobby, 74, 82
Breslaw, Lennie, 11, 64
Brisbane, 153
Broadway, New York, 40, 126
Brookmeyer, Bob, 79, 134, 152
Brown, Clifford, 35, 64
Brown, Les, 14
Brown, Sandy, 27, 72
Brubeck, Dave, 47, 54-6, 71
Brussels, 112

Brymer, Jack, 82-3
Bull's Head, Barnes, 66
Burns, Ralph, 83
Burton, Richard, 99
Busby, Laddie, 38
Bush, Lennie, 123
Butts, Johnny, 83-5
Byers, Billy, 123
Caesar, Sid, 120
Cagney, James, 117-8
Cahn, Sammy, 116
Calloway, Cab, 13-14, 41-3
Calvert, Leon, 21
Cambridge, Freddy, 41-3
Campbell, Gordon, 138
Candoli, Conte, 134
Capitol Records, 92, 109, 144
Carmichael, Hoagy, 40-1
Carnegie Hall, New York, 49
Carney, Harry, 53
Carpenters, 108
Carter, Benny, 140
Castle, Roy, 134, 147
Cater, Pete, 147
Cecil, Malcolm, 64, 70, 72
Chamberlain, Ronnie, 28, 93
Chambers, Paul, 68
Channel 4 (television), 125-6
Chapman, Charles, 12
Charles, Ray, 75-6, 91
Chicago, 27, 137
Chirac, Jacques, 146
Chisholm, George, 36
Christie, Keith, 37-8, 60, 82
Christlieb, Pete, 151
Clare, Alan, 26
Clarke, Kenny, 13-14
Clay, James, 75
Clayton, Buck, 54, 57-8
Clayton, Peter, 59
Clooney, Rosemary, 118

Club Eleven, 20-1, 27, 62
Clyne, Jeff, 56
Cobb, Jimmy, 68
Coe, Tony, 67, 78, 126
Cohn, Al, 61, 80-1, 109, 151
Cole, Natalie, 134
Coleman, Cy, 123
Coltrane, John, 51, 68-9
Columbia Records, 92
Concord Records, 125
Condon, Eddie, 27
Conover, Willis, 54, 57-8
Conti, Bill, 83
Conway, Lennie, 11
Corea, Chick, 80
Costa, Don, 92, 94
Cottler, Irv, 92, 96
Cotton Club, Harlem, 41
Courtley, Bert, 52, 58, 64
Coward, Noel, 94
Craig, Jay, 133
Creese, Malcolm, 139-40
Crescendo magazine, 16, 76
Critchinson, John, 154
Crombie, Tony, 20-2, 42
Crosby, Bing, 71, 115, 118-9, 124
Cuba, 152
Dachau, 16
Dagley, Chris, 147
Daily Express, 103
Daniels, Eddie, 152
Dankworth, John, 20-1, 27, 35, 42,
   60, 65, 73-5, 78, 82-4, 93, 107,
   129, 133
Davis Jr, Sammy, 104, 146
Davis, Bette, 115
Davis, Miles, 20-1, 34, 51, 59,
   64-5, 67-9, 71
Davison, Harold, 40, 52, 54, 67,
   75, 91, 102
Day, Doris, 117, 147

De Franco, Buddy, 21, 149, 152
de Koenigswater, Baroness Nica, 20
de Paul, Gene, 139
Decca Records, 69
Dee, Brian, 64-5, 69-70, 72, 147, 154
Dell, Alan, 59
Desmond, Paul, 59, 71
Deuchar, Jimmy, 35, 58, 60-1, 63, 69
Dickens, Charles, 78
Dietrich, Marlene, 107
Dixon, Iain, 132-3, 138, 150
Dollimore, Ralph, 26
Dorsey, Tommy, 103
Downey, Alan, 132
Drinkwater, Cliff, 16
Drury Lane Theatre, London, 123
Dudley, 25
Dunstall, Clive, 147
Eales, Geoff, 154
Egypt, 99-100
Elderfield, Pete, 45
Ellefson, Art, 60, 73, 75
Ellington, Duke, 42, 53, 115, 125-8
Epstein, Brian, 58
Esquire Records, 26
Evans, Bill, 72, 80
Evans, Chris, 109
Eyden, Bill, 46-7, 64, 70
Fairbanks Jr, Douglas, 126-7
Fairweather, Digby, 142
Falkirk, 28
Fame, Georgie, 134
Farmer, Art, 140
Farnon, Robert, 96, 137
Fawkes, Wally, 27
Faye, Alice, 120
Feldman Club, London, 33

Feldman, Marty, 118
Feldman, Victor, 34, 44-5, 155
Fields, W. C., 127
Fitzgerald, Ella, 21, 90
Flamingo Club, London, 32-3, 39, 44, 46, 66, 69, 84
Flanagan, John, 91, 93
Florida Club, London, 33
Forgie, Barry, 132-3, 138
France, 20, 88, 122
Frantic Five, 28
Frazier, Joe, 67
Gaines, Will, 128
Ganley, Allan, 33-4, 37, 44, 60, 64, 85-6, 92, 101, 108, 122, 140, 149
Garner, Errol, 60
Geneva, 97
George, Bernie, 131-3
Germany, 6, 15-16, 18, 74, 95, 104, 139
Gershwin, George, 9, 30, 152
Getz, Stan, 44, 50-1, 54, 71, 80, 92, 149-52
Gillespie, Dizzy, 13-14, 20-1, 54-5, 57-8, 61
Golders Green Hippodrome, London, 131
Golson, Benny, 134
Gonella, Nat, 15, 41
Gonsalves, Paul, 53
Goodliffe family, 8
Goodman, Benny (clarinet), 10, 13-15, 21, 27, 70
Goodman, Benny (drums), 41, 45
Gordon, Dexter, 80
Gordon, Tom, 138
Gormé, Eydie, 101
Gosport, 41, 72
Gotti, John, 125
Gower, Patrick, 81
Graham, Kenny, 30

Graham, Victor, 16
Grant, Cary, 143
Granz, Norman, 36, 54
Green, Benny, 59, 71, 129-30
Greenwich Village, New York, 51
Gretna Green, Scotland, 57
Griffin, Johnny, 81, 150
Grosvenor House Hotel, London, 90
Haley, Bill, 79
Hall, Henry, 132
Hall, Tony, 44, 69
Hamburg, 110
Hamer, Ian, 51, 55-6, 58
Hamilton, Scott, 125
Hampton, Lionel, 10
Hancock, Herbie, 80
Harlem, New York, 13, 41, 53
Harriott, Joe, 36, 65
Harris, Kenny, 83-5
Harris, Max, 38
Hartley, Bob, 126-8
Harvey, Eddie, 74
Hastings, Jimmy, 132
Hawkins, Coleman, 24
Hawthorne, Nigel, 123
Hayes, Tubby, 11, 24-6, 37, 39, 44-6, 63-9, 76, 78, 80-1, 85, 149-50, 155
Heath, Edward (Prime Minister), 135-6
Heath, Ted (bandleader), 12, 20, 23, 28, 37, 63, 147
Heimann, Paul, 12, 19, 137
Henderson, Joe, 151
Henriques, Basil, 10
Henry Wood Hall, London, 97
Herman, Woody, 10, 39, 115, 152
Hillary, Edmund, 32
Hines, Earl, 13
Hitchcock, Nigel, 150

Hodges, Johnny, 53
Holiday, Billie, 20, 39
Holland, 74, 82
Holly, Buddy, 79
Hope, Bob, 94-5, 115, 119-20, 143
Horler, John, 132, 154
Horne, Lena, 109
Humphries, Skip and Di, 153
Hyman, Phyllis, 126
Iceland, 28-30
India, 126
Innes, Don, 147
Iran, 100-1
Ireland, 100-1, 119
Isaacs, Ike, 19
Israel, 88, 100-1
Italy, 86-8, 98, 101, 122
Jackson, Jack, 44
Jacobs, David, 59, 93
James, Harry, 103, 144
Jazz at the Philharmonic, 36, 54
Jazz Committee, 64
Jazz Couriers, 45-6, 62, 64-5, 149
Jazz Five, 47, 64-6
Jazz from Carnegie Hall, 54
Jazz from Newport, 54, 68, 72
Jazz News, 69
Jazz Today tours, 36
Jazzmakers, 64
Johnson, J. J., 54
Johnson, Judy, 24, 29-30
Johnson, Laurie, 38
Jones, Dill, 24, 29-30, 33, 37, 70
Jones, Jack, 108
Jones, John Rhys, 147
Jones, Quincy, 106-7
Joseph, Julian, 152
Keats, Gordon, 132
Keel, Howard, 113-14
Kellaway, Roger, 56

Kelly, Grace, 95, 100
Kelly, Wynton, 65, 68
Kennedy, John F., 79
Kenton, Stan, 27, 81, 138
Kern, Jerome, 9, 30, 152
Kerr, Anthony, 138
King, Bertie, 37
King, Pete, 62, 80, 129-30
King, Peter, 63, 78, 107, 134, 150
Kinsey, Tony, 44, 82
Kirk, Roland, 67
Kirkcaldy, 28
Klee, Harry, 92
Klein, Harry, 26, 29-30, 47, 63, 65-70, 72, 109, 130
Krall, Diana, 79, 134
Kruger, Jeff and Sam, 32, 39
La Barocca restaurant, London, 123
Laine, Cleo, 73, 78, 93, 95
Lamb, Bobby, 126
Lamont, Duncan, 82, 93
Land, Harold, 51
Lang, Don, 28
Langhorn, Gordon, 27
Lansdowne Studios, London, 37, 41, 82
Las Vegas, 89-90
Lawrence, Steve, 101
Le Sage, Bill, 41, 44
Lee, Peggy, 109, 124
Leicester, 7, 32
Lewis, Jerry, 114
Lewis, Jerry Lee, 79
Lewis, John, 21
Lewis, Vic, 27-8, 30, 33, 51, 58, 60-1, 64
Liberace, 108
Lightfoot, Terry, 65
Lithuania, 1-2
Liverpool Empire, 46

London,
    East End, 1-8, 10-15, 19, 23, 64, 97, 125
    Hammersmith, 76, 82, 92
    Maida Vale, 67, 88, 119, 131
    New Cross, 43
    Soho, 62, 66, 123
    Stamford Hill, 28, 36
London Palladium, 108, 110, 112, 118, 125
Lord, Stan, 81
Lotis, Dennis, 147
Loussier, Jacques, 126
Lowy, Simon, 139
Loxham, Keith, 139
Lubbock, Jeremy, 142
Lugosi, Bela, 98-9
Lusher, Don, 93, 102
LWT (television), 153
Lyttleton, Humphrey, 52, 59
MacBean, George, 25
MacDonald, Alan, 24
MacLaine, Shirley, 16, 112-14
Madrid, 100
Mafia, 103-4, 124-5
Maida Vale Studios, London, 119, 131
Major, John, 96
Mance, Junior, 56
Manchester, 25, 113
Mandel, Johnny, 142
Mann, Tony, 64
Mantooth, Frank, 134
Mapleton Hotel, London, 32
Marquee Club, London, 33, 66, 84
Martin, Barry, 16
Martin, Dean, 114
Martin, George, 107
Marx Brothers, 108
Mathewson, Ron, 46-7

Mathis, Johnny, 111
Matz, Peter, 111
May, Billy, 27, 92, 143-5
May, Tina, 134
McDermott, Galt, 73
McDonald, Al, 26
McDougall, Ian, 73
McDowall, Bob, 139
McGill, Howard, 133, 150
McKenzie, Henry, 27
McNair, Harold, 67
Mecca Ballrooms, 49
Melly, George, 57
Melodisc Records, 37
Melody Maker, 26-7, 34, 39, 63, 72-3, 76
Mendelssohn, Felix, 2
Mercer, Johnny, 116
Milan, 98, 100, 146
Miller, Bill, 92, 96-7
Miller, Glenn, 12, 27, 34, 143-4
Milne, David, 26
Mincer, Bob, 133
Minevitch, Borrah, 92
Minnelli, Liza, 83, 104, 110-11, 146
Mobley, Hank, 51, 70
Modern Jazz Quartet, 43, 71
Monk, Thelonious, 13, 15, 51
Monro, Matt, 70, 90
Montagu, Lord, 65
Moore, Dudley, 60
Moore, Pete, 124-5
Moore, Roger, 96
Moss, Danny, 73
Mostin, Dave, 147
Mountbatten, Louis, 94
Mulder, Bill, 89
Murfitt family, 7
Murray, Anne, 108

Musicians' Union, 20, 32, 39, 49, 54, 114
Nance, Ray, 53
Napper, Kenny, 74
Nash, Nigel, 132
National Jazz Federation, 36, 44
National Youth Jazz Orchestra, 150
Navarro, Fats, 35
Nelson, Oliver, 107
New Musical Express, 30
New York, 20, 48-9, 56, 58, 60, 62, 64, 80, 134, 136-7
Newman, David, 75
Newport Jazz Festival tour, 54-8
Newport, Rhode Island, 54, 56, 60
Newton, Dave, 140
Nightingale, Mark, 150
Nixa Records, 37-8
Nunn, Marjorie, 144, 147
O'Brien, Pat, 117
O'Higgins, Dave, 150
Paris, 75, 112, 146
Parker, Charlie, 13-15, 20, 36, 49, 55, 61, 71, 73, 91, 118
Parkinson, Michael, 59, 114-19
Parlophone Records, 14, 26, 40
Parnell, Jack, 63
Parsons, Tony, 141
Patrick, Johnny, 114
Pearce, John, 154
Pearson, Dave, 56
Peaslee, Richard, 81
Peck, Gregory, 96, 146
Pena, Ralph, 92
Pendleton, Harold, 36, 40, 44
Perelman, S. J., 118
Pericoli, Emilio, 86-8
Peterson, Oscar, 90, 115
Philips Studios, London, 78

Phillips, Phil, 90
Piccadilly Theatre, London, 123
Porcupine Studios, London, 140
Porter, Cole, 9, 152
Presencer, Gerard, 36, 150
Presley, Elvis, 79
Preston, Denis, 37, 41, 82
Price, Charlie, 114
Princess Hotel, Bermuda, 83-4, 87, 89
Queen Mary, 20, 48
Quilley, Denis, 123
Race, Steve, 36, 71
Radio Times, 142
Reece, Dizzy, 44, 69
Rendell, Don, 43, 64
Reykjavik, 30
Rhodes, Burt, 90
Rich, Buddy, 61, 115, 133
Richard, Little, 79
Richards, Emil, 92
Riddle, Nelson, 92
Roach, Max, 64
Robinson, Barry, 132
Robinson, Dougie, 93
Robson, Phil, 138
Rogers, Gingers, 9
Rogers, Johnny, 21
Rolling Stones, 79
Rollins, Sonny, 34, 44, 80, 140
Rome, 122
Ronnie Scott's Club, London, 62-3, 67, 80-1, 129-30
Rose, Denis, 149
Roselli, Jimmy, 124-5
Ross, Annie, 82
Ross, Ronnie, 43, 60, 64, 78, 93
Rotterdam, 146
Roy, Leon, 29-30
Royal Albert Hall, London, 49, 102, 110, 155

Royal Festival Hall, London, 44-5, 49, 92-3, 102, 145, 154-5
Rushing, Jimmy, 54, 57-8
Russo, Bill, 81-2
Sadat, Mrs Anwar, 99
Salisbury Cathedral, 134
Sandoval, Arturo, 152
Sardelli, Nelson, 88-9
Sassoon, Vidal, 10
Savoy Hotel, London, 41, 97
Scales, Prunella, 123
Scotland, 25, 57-58
Scott, Johnny, 51, 67
Scott, Ronnie, 11, 19-22, 27, 28-30, 39, 42, 44-5, 62-3, 65, 67, 78, 80, 83, 90, 115, 126-7, 129-30, 136, 149-50, 155
Scott, Tom, 151
Seamen, Phil, 29, 35, 37-8, 41, 63, 149
Shakespeare, William, 40, 78
Shannon, Terry, 43, 45, 63
Sharon, Ralph, 109-10
Shaw, Artie, 13-14, 135
Shaw, Hank, 21
Shearing, George, 53, 136-7
Shepherd, Dave, 27
Shepherds Bush Empire, London, 120
Sheraton Hotel, London, 97
Sherman, Cyril, 50
Shorter, Wayne, 151
Silver, Horace, 44, 64
Silvers, Phil, 116-118
Sims, Zoot, 42, 51, 54, 61, 73, 79-81, 151
Sinatra Music Society, 144-7
Sinatra, Frank, 26, 34, 50, 71, 91-106, 109, 111, 113-16, 119, 124, 140, 144-7, 154

Sinatra Jr, Frank, 96, 98-9, 102, 145-6
Siptak, George, 18
Skeat, Bill, 89
Skidmore, Alan, 90
Skidmore, Jimmy, 24-6
Sleep, Wayne, 128
Smith, Derek, 37-8, 44
Smith, Mike, 133, 135
Snell, David, 78
Sondheim, Stephen, 136
South Africa, 79
Squires, Rosemary, 134-5, 147
St Martin in the Fields, London, 129
St Paul's Cathedral, London, 125
Stapleton, Cyril, 132
Starr, Ringo, 107
Steele, Tommy, 66
Steiger, Rod, 126-7
Stephenson, Ronnie, 74
Stitt, Sonny, 36, 54, 68-9
Stobart, Kathy, 52
Stokes, Sammy, 37-8, 41
Stoneham, Harry, 59, 115, 120
Streisand, Barbra, 111
Studio 51 club, London, 33
Sullivan, Maxine, 40
Surman, John, 126
Sweden, 20
Swinfield, Ray, 93
Swingle Singers, 126
Sydney, 129
Talbot, Jamie, 150
Talk of the Town, London, 37, 89-90
Tatum, Art, 13, 20
Taylor, Geoff, 26
Taylor, Shaw, 81
Tempo Records, 44, 69
Ternent, Billy, 92

Terry, Clark, 79
Thompson, Eddie, 33, 63
Thompson, Lucky, 79-80
Thorne, Ken, 27
Tolley, Albert, 66
Tormé, Mel, 95, 109, 134, 136
Toronto, 137
Tracey, Stan, 15-16, 19, 23, 26, 37, 42-3, 126, 150
Tracy, Sheila, 133-5
Trocadero Club, London, 92
Turner, Bruce, 36
Turpin, Randolph, 32
Two Is Club, London, 66
TWW (television), 70
Van Doren, Mamie, 144
Van Heusen, Jimmy, 116
Vaughan, Sarah, 15
Victor, Carl, 74
Vienna, 113
Viljalhms, Elly, 30
Village Vanguard, New York, 64
Viola, Al, 92
Voice of America, 54
Warner, Pete, 131
Warren, Harry, 152
Wasser, Stan, 29-30
Watson, Bobby, 134
Watson, Jim, 138
Wayne, John, 118
Webster, Ben, 80
Wein, George, 54
Welles, Orson, 114
Wellins, Bobby, 11, 78
Wells, Dicky, 58
West, Timothy, 123
Wheeler, Kenny, 35, 43, 58-9, 72-3, 81, 126
Whigham, Jiggs, 138
Whiteman, Paul, 151
Whittle, Tommy, 43, 58

Williams, Joe, 52-3
Williams, Martin, 133, 150
Williams, Pat, 108
Williams, Pete, 41
Willox, Roy, 89, 93
Windmill Theatre, London, 18
Winters, Mike and Bernie, 10
Wonder, Stevie, 64
Wood, Andy, 138
Woods, Phil, 72, 79
World War Two, 4, 6-8, 13, 16, 32,
    34, 79, 92, 143
Wray, Ken, 26, 28, 37
Wright, Leo, 56
Wylie, Joe, 83-5
Yorkshire Television, 126
Young, Lester, 13, 20, 50
ZBM Radio, Bermuda, 85
Zito, Torrie, 109

Join the Northway Books mailing list to receive details of new books about jazz, as well as events and special offers. Write to Northway at 39 Tytherton Road, London N19 4PZ or email info@northwaybooks.com

We do not pass information from our mailing list to other organisations.

Doggin' Around

by Alan Plater

with illustrations by the author

2006   £6.99

Described by the author as: 'memoirs of a jazz-crazed play-wright – some of the stories are autobiographical and some of them are true.'

'Rich throughout with smart lines and offbeat observations,' *Guardian*.

'A very, very, readable book,' Michael Parkinson, Radio 2.

'Terrific price, terrific read. It kept me turning pages like mad,' Campbell Burnap.

'Masterly in its knowledge and poetic communication... Don't hang about, go out and buy it,' *Jazz Journal*.

'Illustrated by some extremely funny cartoons... and imbued with the humane wisdom that has made him famous...' www.vortexjazz.co.uk

212 pages

ISBN 09550908 0 6

A History of Jazz in Britain 1919-50
by Jim Godbolt

revised edition with new illustrations throughout.

2005   hardback, £16.99

This book covers the visits of American trail-blazing artists
of the twenties and thirties, their influence on British musicians, the emergence of specialist magazines, rhythm clubs,
discographers and pundits, and the fascinating cloak-and-
dagger plots to defy the Musicians' Union ban.

'As breezy as a riverboat shuffle, ever on the lookout for the
preposterous detail and the opportunity for raffish reminis-
cence,' *Times Literary Supplement.*

'Enlivened throughout by the author's passion for the music
itself and his sharp eye for human failings,' George Melly.

'If you have not bought this book, I urge you to do so – now!'
Humphrey Lyttelton, BBC *Sounds of Jazz.*

285 pages

ISBN 09537040 5 X

Other Books about Jazz
Published by Northway

Ronnie Scott with Mike Hennessey
Some of My Best Friends Are Blues

Alan Robertson
Joe Harriott – Fire in His Soul

Coleridge Goode and Roger Cotterrell
Bass Lines: A Life in Jazz

Peter Vacher
Soloists and Sidemen: American Jazz Stories

Harry Gold
Gold, Doubloons and Pieces of Eight

Digby Fairweather
Notes from a Jazz Life

Ron Brown with Digby Fairweather
Nat Gonella – A Life in Jazz

Forthcoming Books about Jazz

Black British Swing: The African Diaspora's Contribution to England's Own Jazz of the 1930s and 1940s by Andy Simons

Autobiographies by John Chilton and Peter King

A biography of Hank Mobley by Derek Ansell

The republication of Jim Godbolt's hilarious memoir, *All This and Many a Dog*

Musical limericks by Ron Rubin